MAYDAY

MAYDAY

A SAGA OF THE BIG MOTHERS

JW JONES

Charleston, SC
www.PalmettoPublishing.com

Mayday
A Saga of the Big Mothers

Copyright © 2023 by JW Jones

All rights reserved

No portion of this book may be reproduced, stored in a retrieval system, or transmitted in any form by any means– electronic, mechanical, photocopy, recording, or other– except for brief quotations in printed reviews, without prior permission of the author.

First Edition

Hardcover: 979-8-8229-1068-3
Paperback: 979-8-8229-1069-0
eBook: 979-8-8229-1070-6

NON SIBI
SED PATRIAE

NOT FOR SELF,
BUT FOR COUNTRY

CONTENTS

Glossary xv
Preface. xxxi
Chapter 1   Black Knights to the Rescue 1
Chapter 2   In The Beginning. 18
Chapter 3   Sar Det Alpha Keeps Rolling 34
Chapter 4   Ron Clarke's Wild Ride 44
Chapter 5   Fai Tsi Long Again 56
Chapter 6   Continued Success 65
Chapter 7   Shining Brass 82
Chapter 8   Diversions 95
Chapter 9   The End Is in Sight 107
Chapter 10 Prepare for the Next Westpac. . . 116
Chapter 11 Sad Days in Csar 132
Chapter 12 Sar Peaks and Valleys 141
Chapter 13 The Saga at Phu Ly. 153
Chapter 14 Hs-6 Returns 169
Chapter 15 Final Csar Days for
            the Indians. 182
Chapter 16 Operation Formation Star 201
Chapter 17 Hs-6 Crewmen Shine
            in Hc-7 217

Chapter 18	Hs-6 Crew Closeout Their Duties With the Sea Devils ... 242
Chapter 19	The Frank E Evans Incident ... 254
Chapter 20	Tidbits of a Memory Beginning To Fail............ 267

To say thank you for all the help, support, unwarranted and undeserved affection from my family for this tottering old geezer to pursue his passion to bring a spotlight on men he was privileged to have served besides so many years ago, seems miniscule.

Thank you to my daughter Jo Ann, simply the best thing that ever happened in my life and her continued love and encouragement. Thank you to her husband, my son by marriage, Charles, and the love that he shares with his family, my grandson, James, and granddaughter Charlese.

Thank you to Rick Grant, an officer I admired while I served and a friend I look up to today. Rick, Captain Grant, was there at the very start, serving with Sar Det Alpha. He would be the first to draw fire attempting to save a life. He wouldn't be the last.

Thanks to Rick Risher and his wonderful research and dedication to our story of combat search and rescue as he keeps our saga alive for Wings of Gold magazine. He is writing a series about the combat search and rescue during the Vietnam War for the Association of Naval Aviators.

To my old friend Terry Hall, who may have a statue of him found across the bridge in Olongapo City. Terry flew various missions, including flying oxygen breathing apparatus's to the Oriskany. His loyalty to the legacy of the squadron is unquestioned.

A special thank you needs to be extended to Tom Phillips and George Galdorisi and the monumental tome on Combat Search and Rescue, *Leave No Man Behind*. Tom, I enjoyed our conversations at our reunions and am saddened by your passing and the fact that we no longer have you with us. Thank you for encouraging me to undertake this task.

Ken Burns, for maintaining our squadron site, Raunchy Redskins, and your tireless efforts at our reunions. You keep our memories alive.

Ron Milum, a tireless historian recording and documenting HC 7 history for the past many decades. His selfless work is truly a labor of dedication to the memory of his squadron and all who served.

Thanks to my pilot, Vern von Sydow, who showed daily what leadership was. I was with Mr. von Sydow in a few tense moments, from trying to find a cloud to hide our helo during a MIG alert to leading a rescue disregarding the heavy artillery fire that had his crew bracketed. I never saw fear. Vern, you have made everyone you have contact with, better by your presence.

Thanks to Al Fox. Who became our last combat skipper. Your dedication, humor, caring spirit, made a tough job much better. I am sad you are gone but skipper your life mattered.

Thank you to the wonderful kids I have taught and coached since those heady days. My time with you have taught me that our sacrifices were worth it. You have shown me that our nation still has the necessary ingredients to continue to be "that city on the hill," that we were promised four centuries prior. For those that wish to complain about the kids today, well they have not met the ones I have been fortunate enough to have in my life.

I think of my childhood friends, Mike, Terry, Jack, and Jene and I think they believed I would be the last person to try to author a book. In truth they thought I would also be the last person to read a book. Jene went on to serve his country in Mike Company 3/7th Marines while Mike served as airbase security in the Republic of Vietnam.

George Armstrong, a Blackfoot from Idaho, who would burst into "Hail to the Redskins" as his Washington football team was playing my Cowboys. A true warrior that defended his crew with steadfast courage. Crazy Pigeon, I miss my time with you.

Bernie Riley and Ski with an N, it was always an adventure every liberty call. You never disappointed, your fights on liberty were epic and would always end as they started, with your friendship, and the battle would always recommence the next liberty with Bernie predicting but never achieving victory.

Leonard Gonerka, I remember the last time I saw you, in a stokes stretcher on the flight deck. Bullet still in your leg and the piece of armor plating in the other leg, just prior to us airlifting you to the Danang military hospital. I remember when the Admiral asked what he could do for you and your reply of a bottle of Scotch and a beautiful blonde, and if memory serves, he did find you a bottle of Scotch, mission fifty percent complete on his part.

I would like to thank the littles, those elementary school children on every campus who made this old man feel wanted. I was happy and proud to have been your honorary grandfather.

Thanks to Mickey Miller and Mike Clifton, for allowing me to enter the teaching and coaching profession at my late time in life. Don Waddle my old coaching compadre, I still envy you. It takes greatness to have a Mama's Place Burrito named in your honor.

Thank you to the wonderful woman, who did not spare the red ink while editing and proofreading this project, Ms. Olabami Daniels.

For the reader, please accept my apologies, no one could do these wonderful men justice and their unselfish risk of their lives and future, trying to rescue another American. I have often been asked by my students, "Coach, if you knew how Vietnam would turn out, would you still go?"

My answer then and now, "If I could serve with the same men again, I would go in a heartbeat, for they were the finest men I ever knew."

Most of all thanks to those wonderful guys that would strap on a parachute, climb into a plane, be cat shot off a carrier and fly into the jaws of hell daily. You showed all of us that courage is more than a word in a spelling bee, for you, it was a way of life. We, in the rescue services are sorry we could not bring all of you home.

GLOSSARY

Unless the reader was blessed to be a rotor head, a certain lexicon of our language may be in order. And if you are a rotor head, feel free to nip on nectar and feed on ambrosia, you are truly one of the chosen ones.

AAA: Anti-Aircraft Artillery

AD: Naval enlisted classification for aviation mechanic. ADJ was the jet mechanic designation, ADR designated aircraft engine mechanic for reciprocal engines. A number 3,2,1, or C would follow it to show rank. Petty Officer 3rd class, Petty Officer 2nd Class, Petty Officer 1st Class, or Chief Petty Officer.

Air-to-ground: A weapon designed to be delivered from the air to ground targets.

Aircraft Designations. The USN, US Army, and USAF established a joint aircraft designation system in the early 1960's. Prior to this all three systems had their own designations, and the same type of aircraft may have totally different designators i.e., the C-47 cargo aircraft in the air force was known as the R4D in the Navy. The first letter was mission type, in this case C for cargo the number was vehicle number, etc. The F-8, was F for fighter, 8 vehicle number, an RF-8 was the same type of aircraft but modified for Reconnaissance (RF)

AMS: Navy enlisted classification to designate an aviation structural mechanic. A number 3,2,1, or C would follow it to show rank. Petty Officer 3rd class, Petty Officer 2nd Class, Petty Officer 1st Class, or Chief Petty Officer.

AT: Navy enlisted designation for avionics technician. ATN-Navigation, ATR-Radar. A number 3,2,1, or C would follow it to show rank. Petty Officer 3rd class, Petty Officer 2nd Class, Petty Officer 1st Class, or Chief Petty Officer.

GLOSSARY

AX: Navy enlisted designation for aviation antisubmarine warfare technician. A number 3,2,1, or C would follow it to show rank. Petty Officer 3rd class, Petty Officer 2nd Class, Petty Officer 1st Class, or Chief Petty Officer.

B40: North Vietnamese clone of the RPG-2 Soviet rocket propelled grenade

Bandit: Call alerting aircraft of enemy aircraft. Usually, MIG fighters. See Bullseye call.

Big Mother: Call sign for the SH 3A rescue helicopters, later designated armored HH-3A helos.

Bullseye Call: Used to denote location of enemy aircraft. Bullseye was a North Vietnamese location, normally a city. Radio call would start with BANDIT…BANDIT, followed with BULLSEYE, a line of bearing, and a distance. For example, if the Bullseye was Hanoi, the call BANDIT. BANDIT, BULLSEYE 335, 65 NAUTICAL would mean an enemy aircraft is 335 degrees (NNW) 60 nautical miles from Hanoi center. The bullseye city would be changed daily.

BM: Abbreviation for Big Mother in many logs and histories.

CA: Navy identifier for a heavy cruiser. Main battery was nine eight-inch main guns.

Charlie: Name given to the insurgent communists in South Vietnam. Name comes from the phonetic pronunciation for VC, Victor Charles. Sometimes called Chuck. Although Charlie was sometimes used for the North Vietnamese, these were normally referred to with their phonetic pronunciation, November Victors. They was no hard and fast rule, and these terms would change with time, unit, and individually.

CL: Navy identifier for a light cruiser with main batteries of six-inch guns.

CLG: Same as above but armed with missiles.

Crab Crusher: Nickname for the HU-16 Albatross, amphibious airplane.

CSAR: Acronym for Combat Search and Rescue

CV: Letters followed by a number indicated an aircraft carrier. The third letter indicated type, CVE-escort carrier, CVA-attack carrier, CVS-antisubmarine carrier normally an Essex Class platform with hydraulic catapults (Essex Class with steam catapults could launch larger aircraft and were usually attack carriers for example Oriskany et al.

CVN-denoted nuclear-powered carrier, although during the Vietnam War the Enterprise CVN-65 is the only carrier with that power plant. The west coast had four CVS carriers USS Hornet (HS 2 & air group), USS Yorktown (HS-4 & air group),USS Bennington (HS-8 & air group) and USS Kearsarge (HS-6 & air group)

DD: Followed by a number, indicates a destroyer. Main gun usually a 5-inch 38 caliber.

DE: Followed by a number indicates a destroyer escort. Main gun usually a 3 inch.

Dixie Station: USN forces in the Gulf of Tonkin below the DMZ, east of South Vietnam.

DL or **DLG**: Destroyer Leader also known as a frigate, later reclassified as a cruiser. The G designation denotes guided missile.

DMZ: Demilitarized Zone established when the Geneva Conference in 1954 to separate North and South Vietnam. The line was roughly along the 17th parallel.

Feet Dry: A radio call from an aircrew that indicated the aircraft was overland, in this case North Vietnam.

Feet Wet: A radio call indicating the aircraft was over the relative safety of the Gulf of Tonkin.

Fansong: Fire control radar developed by the Soviets and furnished to the People's Army of North Vietnam. First units engaged were known as Fansong Bravo, where this radar could discriminate with the target if the target was above 500 feet. Fansong Charlie, was similar except it could engage targets down to 300 feet. It was used both by radar guided AAA and SA-2 surface to air missiles.

FLAK: Air burst from anti-aircraft cannon that would result in an overpressure near the burst with corresponding shrapnel. Name comes from World War 2 Germany, <u>F</u>lieger <u>A</u>bwer <u>K</u>annonen.

HAC: Helicopter Aircraft Commander. While the helo was in flight, his word was law regardless of rank.

Harbor Master: Command and control call sign of USN search and rescue commander in the Gulf.

HC: HC-1, HC-7. Helicopter Combat Support Squadron. Multiple roles from vertical replenishment, SAR, aerial mine sweeping, plane guard, etc. HC-1, in early 1967, prior to HC-3, HC-1, had a composition of 1,200 officers and men in detachments throughout the Pacific. HC-7, upon its founding in 1967 would assume the combat search and rescue role in Vietnam.

HH-3A: Sikorsky S-61 model helo that had been modified by the addition of self-sealing tanks, armored pilot seats, removal of sonar equipment, armored hydraulic closet, armor plating on engines, transmission, and gear boxes. The front entrance hatchway was removed and am armored plated gun mount installed. In the cabin at the hoist station/cargo door a Dutch door type gun mount was installed.

HH-3E: Sikorsky S-61 type helo that had been purposefully built for rescue. Armor plated, self-sealing tanks, the rescue hoist was located closer to the front of the helo allowing better visibility for the pilot. Landing gear sponsons were placed aft of the hoist/gunner station allowing a better field of fire forward for the gunner/hoist operator. Did have more limited fire aft. The Air Force did not place guns on these aircraft until 1967.

HS: HS-2, HS-4, HS-6, HS-8, HS-10. Helicopter squadrons trained in antisubmarine warfare. Flew the SH-3A variant of the Sikorsky S-61 airframe during the time of this book.

Indian Gal: Normal radio call sign of HS-6

Jesus Nut: A mythical mechanical part of a helicopter that if it failed would cause catastrophic failure of the airframe, ergo the crew would meet Jesus.

Jolly Green: Call sign of HH-3E rescue helicopters used by the ARRS (aerospace rescue and recovery squadrons).

LPH: Landing Platform Helicopter. A large ship used to launch and recover helicopters. Early in the war, escort carriers surplus from WW2 were used in this role. Today a well deck has been added to facilitate the launching of assault boats. **LPHD** (Landing Platform Helo Dock) the modern Kearsarge is one of these ships.

M-16: Personal weapon that could be used in both the semi and fully automatic mode. Magazine held 20 rounds but were usually filled with 17 to prevent jamming. 5.56mm NATO round. Carried on SAR helos as a personal defense weapon in case the helo was downed in enemy territory.

M-60: Machine gun, gas operated, partially developed from the German MG42 of WW2. It fired 7.62x51mm ammunition at a cyclic rate of 9-11 rounds per second. The ammunition was linked. The gun was prone to jamming by the fouling of the barrel by heavy use.

M-79: 40mm grenade launcher known as the Thumper or the Blooper. Range limited to 400 yards at maximum elevation making it of limited use in helos.

Martin-Baker Seat: An ejection system whereas the pilot would initiate the ejection sequence by pulling face curtain et al., followed by the canopy releasing, rocket igniting at the bottom of the seat to propel pilot clear of tail assembly. A bladder in the seat back would inflate to push pilot from the Martin Baker seat prior to chute canopy deploying. A safety key with fabric tail would be placed in seat to prevent the seat from inadvertently firing by accident when a plane captain or other maintainer may pull curtain by accident.

Mayday: Universal call given by an aircraft in trouble.

MIGCAP: An aircraft missioned to guard other missions, attack, rescue, etc. against potential enemy fighter attacks by MIG aircraft. Mig Combat Air Patrol.

North Sar: Usually a DLG, later classified as a Cruiser, somewhere near the Haiphong Harbor. Search and Rescue designated ship for the Northern Gulf of Tonkin.

Pigeons: A request for direction and distance to friendly home base (ship or shore station), akin to a pigeon homing to its nest. Would be given, "Big Mother 71, request pigeons to Grey Eagle (USS Ranger)."

PIRAZ: Acronym for Positive Radar Identification Zone. A ship that tracked all air traffic in the Gulf and North Vietnam. It also controlled all air strikes by the navy against North Vietnamese assets. It's radio call sign was Red Crown.

Port: Naval term for left side of ship. Originated in the ancient days prior to a rudder. A steering board was used to steer the vessel and was located on the right side aft of the craft. When the ship docked it protected this vital gear from damage by docking on the left side, the side of the port city.

PR: Navy enlisted designation for parachute rigger. Charged with maintaining personal survival equipment. A number 3,2,1, or C would follow it to show rank. Petty Officer 3rd class, Petty Officer 2nd Class, Petty Officer 1st Class, or Chief Petty Officer.

RESCAP: An aircraft missioned to function as a combat air patrol over rescue aircraft during the rescue phase of the mission. Note, normally not capitalized but will be capitalized in this work as the immense sign of respect we have for these wonderful, brave, pilots. Rescue Combat Air Patrol

RESCORT: An aircraft missioned to escort the rescue craft to the place of rescue. Note, normally not capitalized but will be capitalized in this work as the immense sign of respect we all have for these wonderful, brave, pilots. Rescue Escort

Rotor Heads: Those wonderfully brave and uncommonly handsome men (and today also women) tasked with the flying or maintaining of helicopters. Alternately also known as the coolest people in the world, without exception. When Megan married Prince Harry, she fulfilled every young woman's dream, not to be a princess, but to be married to a helicopter pilot.

Rotary wing: Lifting system of helicopters. Commonly called blades but were wing shaped and produced the lift required for helo flight.

SAM: Surface to air missile. North Vietnam used the Soviet S-75 Dvina missile. NATO code SA-2. The 35-foot-long missile travel more than Mach 3 and delivered a 440-pound warhead that could be command detonated.

SAR: Acronym for Search and Rescue

Scooter: Nickname of the Douglas A-4 Skyhawk, a workhorse of the attack aircraft squadrons.

Shrike: U.S. antiradiation missile designed to degrade anti-aircraft assets. It would follow the enemy radar emissions back to its source using its warhead to destroy the radar site.

Skipper: Term reserved for the commanding officer, whether it was a squadron, tugboat, aircraft carrier, etc. Denoted command.

South Sar: A ship with a helo deck situated just north of a line of bearing north of the DMZ, in the Gulf of Tonkin.

Starboard: Naval term for right side of the ship. In the time before a rudder was invented, a steering board was used to steer the vessel. It was mounted on the right side of the ship, the steer-board side.

Wild Weasel: Term for mission or aircraft that were used to entice SAM or AAA sites to reveal themselves where they could be attacked and degraded. Highly dangerous assignment.

Yankee Station: USN forces in the Gulf of Tonkin, north of the DMZ, east of North Vietnam.

PREFACE

The United States would lose more than 10,000 aircraft in the Vietnam War. To regain the valuable flight crews aboard these aircraft, Combat Search and Rescue had to be developed and honed. In its infancy using what resources were available was paramount. The US Navy needed to employ its antisubmarine squadrons. HS 6 was one of four operational ASW squadrons on the west coast, a fifth, HS-10 was used as a training squadron, with the purpose of being a Replacement Air Group (RAG).

Helicopter Antisubmarine Squadron 6 was morphed from HS 2 in 1956. Originally it was HS 2 Det. N, on board the Essex Class carrier USS Princeton. However, in the summer of 1956, while between Okinawa and Formosa, it became its own entity under the command of LCDR Dougal McKay. The pilots flew the HO4S Helos at the time of commissioning but upon return to the Naval base of NAS Ream field, found in Imperial Beach,

California, soon began transitioning to the HSS 1 (SH34), and assumed its primary mission of defense against the Soviet submarine nuclear armed threat that appeared after the Second World War.

The changing technologies of helicopters, and the new role the squadron had assumed in its ASW role soon saw the HSS1 aircraft get swapped out for the new Sikorsky SH-3A with its AQS 10 dipping sonar.

The crews trained long hours at their new role, using both simulators at NAS North Island, and training flights off the coast. However, in the middle 60s a new reality surfaced: war in Southeast Asia, and with an adversary that did not have submarines. In the closing days of spring, 1966, the squadron was readying itself to board the USS Kearsarge, a 27,000-ton Ticonderoga sub class of the Essex carrier platform, and journey to the Gulf of Tonkin. Crew members that had spent hundreds of hours in simulators and actual flight training were now bussed to NAS North Island for a 4-hour familiarization course on the M60 machine gun. The actual target practice from an aerial platform would happen enroute with the crew tossing a flare into the ocean and the pilots making passes near the flare to allow the former sonar operators, now gunners/hoist operators to adjust to the 100 knot windage. The instructor at NAS North Islands would always say, "First to put rounds on target, will win the day, and be allowed to play again another day."

What was once a cruise to the mysterious Far East, now took on a new urgency.

CHAPTER 1

BLACK KNIGHTS TO THE RESCUE

We all stand on the backs of others; we follow those that go before us and walk in their tracks adjusting our pace as we stride. unknown

The war was in its infancy. Combat Search and Rescue was relearning the lessons from the past with newer equipment, opposed to a foe that was ever evolving.

HS-4, the Black Knights, reported to Yankee Station in late February 1966, relieving HS-2. They would make their time on Yankee Station, the area of the Gulf of Tonkin abutting North Vietnam, very productive with twenty-three recues under their belt.

The air war was unfolding; new techniques and equipment were being developed. Early days of SAR would see the Navy squadrons doing battle with makeshift armament against the North Vietnamese Army, whose tactics and weaponry were improving daily.

Early adjustments included steel plating fabricated by the ships' welding shops coupled with a .30 caliber machine gun with a mount also fashioned by local craftsmen. The early SH-3A aircraft did not sport self-sealing tanks armor plating protecting the hydraulic closet, engines, main gear box, or intermediate gear box. Even armor-plated seats would come later.

Meanwhile, personal equipment came in the form of flak vests. The pilots would wear theirs backwards to be able to shed the heavy gear quickly in case of a water ditching since the Mae West inflatable flotation device would not support the combined weight of the crew member and flak vest.

Command structures for rescues were also implemented alongside their identifying call signs. The Navy normally answered to Harbor Master, usually stationed on a cruiser or a guided missile frigate (DLG) stationed in the Gulf north of the DMZ. They also designated two ships capable of helicopter operations to the permanent stations in the Gulf. The South SAR Station was located between the DMZ and Vinh, while the North SAR Station was near the port of Haiphong. Both stood several miles off the coast as a precaution against MIG attacks, and Soviet-made patrol boats, containing surface to surface missiles.

In late February, the Black Knights North SAR helo had been aloft most of the day and was returning when the distinct sight of strobe lights appeared on the water below. Circling the area, they discovered a total of five USAF crewmen. After hoisting them aboard they learned they were part of a reconnaissance mission and their RB 66C was targeted by a SA 2 surface to air missile. The aircraft, one of 36 of that type produced by Douglas aircraft, had its radio communications destroyed in the attack and was unable to call for help. Their squadron, the 41st Tactical Reconnaissance Squadron, reported they were overdue, but the location of the downed air crew of six was unknown. Unfortunately, while five were plucked from the waters, the sixth crew member, Captain John Causey, remained missing and was presumed lost.

* * *

On Mar 14, an F-4C Phantom from the 480th TFS was hit by antiaircraft fire and the pilot headed for the coast. The pilot and his back seater ejected After reaching "feet wet" (the radio call that showed he was over the Gulf), the pilot and his back seater ejected, parachuting near Hon Gai Island, one of the small islands near the port city of Vinh.

Immediately, an HU 16 amphibious plane from the 37th ARRS, also affectionately known in the Navy wardrooms as a crab crusher, vectored to the area and sighted the two downed crew one mile offshore of the island, with a flotilla of sampans heading towards them. Seeing one of the men was injured, a Para jumper, Airman 1c James Pleiman, swam to the rafts with a rescue hook. The hook would allow the HU 16 to reel in the rafts like a winch hooked to a stranded vehicle.

However, before this could happen, the sampans opened fire on the rescue craft. The crew returned fire with an M16, but that jammed after a few rounds. The navigator worked to clear the weapon and soon got it firing again. When Pleiman and the two downed airmen reached the cabin door, the HU 16 was struck by a 130mm round and exploded upon contact with the aircraft, creating a surge of shrapnel and concussive pressure that killed Pleiman and the radioman, A1c Robert Hilton.

The rest of the crew were left to face a sinking plane, and the flames that ensued from the leaking fuel. An injured Maj. James Pearson, the F4's pilot, would have been killed by the flames had Captain Robert Price, the HU 16 navigator, not pulled him out of harm's way to safety. Meanwhile, the co-pilot, Lt. Hall, grabbed the Flight Engineer, SSgt Clyde Jackson, who had been injured in the explosion, pulling him to safety. Now six men were in the water trying to escape the growing ring of flames.

Fortunately, HS-4 had two crews near the area performing logistic duties. Although they were unarmored, both mounted M-60s and were diverted to the area when they got the first calls of trouble from the F-4 crew.

One of the crews' pilots was Lt. Rick Klippert and the other Lt. (jg) Bill Terry.

Klippert arrived on the scene first. However, while trailing Klippert, Terry observed small arms fire directed at Klippert's crew and ordered his gunners to suppress the fire coming from the sampans. Hose down the junks to suppress the fire. As they fought, a large junk, some 40 meters in length, began to close in on the four men, firing as it approached. Fortunately, they were saved when an A-1 fired a salvo of 2.75-inch air to ground missiles, transforming the junk into flotsam. Upon seeing a fellow craft quickly reduced to floating debris, the rest of the sampan flotilla temporarily lost interest, though small arms fire continued from the shoreline.

To allow Klippert and Terry to remain focused on hoisting the six to safety, the A-1 assisting the rescue constantly strafed the shoreline with 20mm cannon and air to ground rockets.

Klippert hoisted three aboard and radioed that he was full. Terry, on the other hand, experienced a bit of a delay bringing the remaining three aboard as two of them had trouble getting into the horse collar due to their injuries. The delay was utilized by the enemy who directed large rounds towards Terry's hovering bird, raising columns of water that trapped and forced Terry to call the RESCAP aircraft for help. The RESCAP responded that he was out of ammunition but bravely continued to make dry runs on the shore batteries to divert the attention of the gun crews.

Soon, the crewmen had two of the men aboard while one was bleeding profusely from shrapnel wounds the other lay in the troop seat on the port side, suffering from severe back injuries. The hoist operator lowered the sling to the last remaining survivor, but it was to no avail. Rounds continued to fall dangerously close to the H-3. When the hail of shells began gaining on the helo from the rear, the crew in the back advised, "Flight we need to get the f#@# out of here!!!" Immediately, Terry nosed the helo over and broke hover.

Terry decided he would quickly circle the area, allowing time for the shore fire to subside. When it was more advantageous, he would then enter a hover, and execute the rescue. However, as he neared Price, rounds again began to strike where he intended to land, forcing him to break off his attempt.

Auspiciously, an additional RESCAP aircraft began to arrive on the scene with fresh loads of ordinance, and soon went to work attacking the batteries that were hindering the rescue effort.

Terry also learned another helo was on scene: the UH-2 helicopter from HC-1 Det. 5, aboard the USS England, piloted by Lcdr. David McCracken was now available. Soon after the UH-2 helo arrived, more A-4s appeared and began to offload their bombs, rockets, and cannon fire on the enemy. The fire from the shore immediately diminished.

Now out of harm's way, Terry departed with his wounded passengers as McCracken sped towards Price, who was now beyond exhausted. He had engaged the enemy earlier from the HU-16 with an M-16, aided in securing the F-4 crew safely away from the fire surrounding his sinking aircraft, and assisted others in his party while under fire from shore units. At this point, he was at his physical and emotional end. McCracken approached with his co-pilot Ens. Robert Clark, senior crewman AECS Robert Davis and second crewman Airmen Robert Campbell. A few sampans were still in the area and engaged the oncoming helo, but Campbell, with a handheld Thompson sub machine gun, returned fire, killing one of his tormentors. The UH-2, built as a survival aircraft, had a loud hailer and McCracken used this to broadcast to Price to get out of the raft, but the explosion that had killed two of the navigator's crewmen had also broken his ear drums, and he was unable to hear. However, this time, when the sling was let down, he took it and was hoisted to safety. McCracken immediately left the area.

For Price, his heroism did not go unnoticed. He was awarded the Air Force Cross, the nation's second highest award for heroic action, only second to the Medal of Honor. His certificate read:

"Captain Donald S. Price distinguished himself by extraordinary heroism in connection with military operations against an opposing armed force as Navigator aboard an HU-16B aircraft, in the Gulf of Tonkin, offshore of North Vietnam, on 14 March 1966. On that date, Captain Price participated in a successful rescue of the downed crew of an F-4C aircraft, in hostile waters. As they approached the area, the downed crew members were sighted. A determination was made that an open sea landing would be necessary to affect a successful rescue. At this time, a force of approximately 25 motorized sampans were observed heading toward the downed pilots. After a full stall landing was made and while they were maneuvering toward the nearest survivor, a heavy barrage of hostile gun fire was directed at the aircraft from the nearby sampans. Moments later, the aircraft was struck, exploded, and was almost immediately engulfed in flames. As the heat from the fire became intense, the crew was forced to abandon the aircraft. As Captain Price jumped into the water, he encountered the F-4C pilot who had discarded both his life raft and life jacket and

was struggling to remain afloat. Captain Price towed the pilot on his back away from the burning aircraft and continued to render assistance while awaiting rescue. Several minutes later, helicopters arrived on the scene and Captain Price, although in great pain from multiple wounds received in the explosion, remained in the water to complete his mission of rescuing the downed F-4C pilot. He assisted the pilot into a sling and the helicopter departed. Captain Price was now the sole survivor in the water and artillery shells began to fall around him, preventing rescue by another helicopter. As he struggled into a nearby raft, the sampans began converging on him forcing him to re-enter the water and swim seaward. At this time, two F-4C aircraft and a helicopter arrived in the area. While the F-4C's suppressed the hostile fire, the helicopter effected a successful rescue. By his extraordinary heroism, gallantry, and determination, Captain Price has reflected the highest credit upon himself and the United States Air Force."

For A1c Robert Hilton, his courage was recognized posthumously with the Silver Star. A1c

James Pleiman was awarded his second Silver Star, he had earned one four months earlier, the second one sadly was also a posthumous award. His fellow crewmen last observed his lifeless form floating face down. Pleiman's remains were returned by the North Vietnamese following the war. Hiltons remains were not recovered.

* * *

On May 2nd, Lt. R.H. Mansfield of Attack Squadron 212 was making attack runs, when one of his missiles went awry and impacted with his A-4E ten miles from Vinh. He immediately called Mayday and ejected.

Lt. (jg) Dick Benson and crew, co-pilot Lt. (jg) Dennis Daniels, first crew AX2 David Waddell, and second crew of PR1 Russell Hietbrick had been on the South SAR station, orbiting and awaiting the results of the days attacks. So, when Benson heard Mansfield broadcasting from his survival radio, he immediately established contact.

He tried to reassure the stricken pilot he would be on his way as soon as RESCORT arrived, but Mansfield told him it would be a wasted trip as enemy infantry were already closing in on his position.

However, there was a problem. The voice on the radio had not been authenticated. Authentication would consist of a challenge, for instance the word dog, the reply would be one only known by the downed pilot. In the authors file…if dog was the challenge, the reply was Teddy, the name of my childhood dog. These were all kept for rapid authentication. In this case, Attack Squadron 212 would have the challenge and answer. This prevented an English speaker from luring rescue craft into a killing zone or flak trap.

Now Benson had a dilemma. He could follow procedure and await RESCORT and authentication for naught or break procedure and risk his life and crew to save a life from possible death or certain capture. He homed in on the voice on the survival radio with his ADF (automatic direction finder) and soon reported "feet dry" as he passed over the coast into the heavily defended Vinh vicinity.

Soon, he noticed his ADF needle swing, demonstrating he had just flown over Mansfield's position, and immediately turned to execute a hover, while his gunners held off the approaching North Vietnamese with their M-60s. Waddell reported that they were in a small depression and the NVA were all around, including below and above the helo. He also observed that the fire was coming from handheld automatic weapons, mostly AK 47. The fire below and on the same level could be answered, but fire from above required a gunner to shoot through his own rotor blade arc, an event that made him highly unpopular with his pilot and crew.

Regardless, Waddell sent the sling down. But as it approached Mansfield, the enemy infantry began peppering the helicopter repeatedly, hitting one of the three hydraulic systems in the H-3, and rendering it inoperative. Waddell also discovered, to his dismay, that it had also disabled the hoist. When Waddell reported that rounds had hit the hoist and cable, the suppression fire from Benson's crew decreased, they had to man the hoist.

Daniels, on the other hand, was far from being on the better side of the NVA attack. His instrument panel, gauges, and aircraft aluminum were being shattered by small arms fire. And though the panel took some of the velocity away from the small arms fire, it did not stop Daniels from suffering a leg wound in the exchange.

Soon, Benson saw that staying put was not in the missions' best interest. As if on cue, Waddell told his flight station it was time to go even though Mansfield was suspended on a broken hoist, and a cable that could be fraying. Benson nosed the helo over, broke hover and sped to the coast.

Waddell and Hietbrick put Chicago grips on the cable, fastening it to the gun mount in case of a failure. Then Waddell looked down at the pilot suspended 30 feet under the cabin and grinned as the newly rescued pilot had both arms fully extended and gave the enemy both middle fingers as an international greeting of farewell to his tormenters. It offered a moment of levity as two crewmen struggled to hold the fraying steel with their hands, the leather flight gloves being ripped by the fraying wire. The Chicago grips were yet untested, and they wished for them to remain so.

Finally, after arriving at the relative safety of being feet wet, and without an alternative to the damaged hoist, Benson gently lowered the helo, allowing Mansfield to free himself from the sling, and get picked up by a Clementine HC-1 that had sped to the scene.

Benson had broken protocol, but he had saved one of his own. For the crew that rescued him, the image of Mansfield, suspended 30 feet from actual safety, still under heavy fire from North Vietnamese regulars, arms outstretched, with both hands flipping a bird even as the two helo crewmen held the fraying cable, would be long remembered. The defiance in the face of capture or death meant this was a man worth saving, worth the risk. After the adrenaline had subsided, their breathing returned to normal, and bodies began to function, Benson discovered he had a souvenir from the day—one communist slug lodged in his gluteus maximus muscle complex. He had been shot in the butt. A fair exchange for Mansfield's life.

For the Black Knights, Benson and Daniels would be awarded Silver Stars, while Waddell and Hietbrick would be decorated with Distinguished Flying Crosses.

Notes:
Valor: Rescue in the Gulf of Tonkin | Air & Space Forces Magazine (airandspaceforces.com) web
Air Force Cross—Home of Heroes web
Email conversations with David Waddell
Phillips, T and Galdorisi, G. (2008) *Leave No Man Behind*, Zenith Press

CHAPTER 2

IN THE BEGINNING
SAR DET ALPHA

Helicopter Antisubmarine Squadron 4 had been on Westpac since the first of 1966 and it was time for them to rotate back to their home base at NAS Ream Field. Their deployment on the USS Yorktown had been a successful one, as they rescued twenty-four downed aviators.

To relieve HS 4, an advanced detachment of ten officers and 31 enlisted, plus 2 1/2 tons of tools, personal baggage, etc. were flown from California to Hawaii. Upon landing in Hawaii, the five crews plus maintenance staff were given three days without duties. At the end of the liberty period, they met at Barbers Point NAS and boarded an older DC 7 propeller aircraft for their trip to Cubi Point, Republic of the Philippines.

Upon landing at Cubi Point, a car was waiting to take the Detachment Commander,

Warren Lockwood, along with Ron Nichols and Ron Clarke, both pilots, to base operations to secure transportation via a C-1 carrier onboard delivery (COD) aircraft to Yorktown. However, they were informed by the petty officer on duty that though a COD was scheduled to leave within the hour, it was already full. Cdr. Lockwood then handed a copy of orders that said these men were flying at priority one and that others would be bumped from the flight. An hour later, the leaders of Det. Alpha were on their way to the Tonkin Gulf and the USS Yorktown.

Lt. Clarke, as Detachment Maintenance Officer, was given the responsibility to give each armored SAR aircraft a test flight. HS 4 still had a full squadron, along with parts, to help with the repair if any of these birds were found wanting.

To bring the relieving flight crew up to speed, split crew familiarization flights were scheduled, with a pilot from HS 4 joining a pilot from HS 6. The aircrew in the back of the aircraft were also mixed.

On his first familiarization flight, HS-6 pilot Lt. (jg) Rick Grant was paired with Lt. Reid Carlton of HS 4. But what was to be a routine flight turned intense soon after the aircraft arrived at North Sar station. The skipper of Attack Squadron 155 was hit north of Haiphong and was forced to eject near the Fai Tsi Long Islands and these islands were partially staffed with North Vietnamese troops and militia.

The American pilot, Charles Peters, Nebraskan by birth, coaxed his stricken plane until the last moment, and when feet wet, ejected at low altitude, going down among the myriad of islands in the chain. The mixed crew searched fervently for the downed skipper. After a futile search, in which the crew found a helmet bag, pieces of a Nomex style flight suit, and more airplane debris, all amid a school of Hammerhead sharks, it was decided the pilot had been lost to enemy action. However, as the crew exited the area, they were taken under fire by North Vietnamese defenders on the island.

Lt. Carlton gave Grant the order to exit the area. Grant, being used to a more leisurely pace of flying at Ream Field, made a standard turn only to be issued another command by the much more combat experienced Carlton, "Rick, I have the aircraft,"; this was accompanied by a sharp motion on the cyclic and a kick of the rudder to bring the aircraft quickly about. Carlton had been flying combat since the Black Knights of HS 4 were on station. For Grant, it was a quick lesson. and he would soon be applying this familiarization flight curriculum to the rest of his flights in the Tonkin Gulf.

Overhead, an A1 Sky Raider from the 602nd Air Commando Squadron was orbiting the area to provide combat air support for the rescue operation (RESCAP). The Sky Raider, a propeller-powered relic of the Korean War, was a favorite among the Combat Search and Rescue crews due to its ability to get low and slow with the helicopter. However, Major Robert Williams, the pilot was incapacitated when the plane got struck in the canopy area by enemy fire. Both the plane and pilot hit the surface of the water. The Sandie pilot was not seen or heard from again.

This first flight by members of HS 6 in a combat zone foreshadowed the deadly task ahead of them as they relieved the Black Knights of SAR duty in the Gulf of Tonkin.

***

On July 1st, HS 6 Sar Det Alpha assumed the role of combat search and rescue in the Gulf of Tonkin theatre. North Vietnam was divided into ten rescue zones. The four zones in the coastal areas were to be assigned to the naval assets, while the 5 zones in the eastern part of North Vietnam and the zone along the DMZ (whoever continued to call this the Demilitarized Zone had a sarcastic streak) were assigned to the Air Force. Call signs were assigned according to aircraft types. Pedro was given to the HH 43 crews, Jolly Green to the Air Force HH 3E crews, Clementine to the H2 (Hooky Two) crews, and Big Mother to the HH 3A crews of the Navy.

During their time on Yankee Station, the squadron would normally send a bird aloft prior to the first attack launch of the day. This bird would continue to the North SAR

Station, usually a destroyer of DLG close to the coast near Haiphong. This Helo would circle the area, awaiting the "Mayday, Mayday" call, which signified that one of the members of the attack flights was having trouble.

Without this call and the ensuing coordination with the rescue coordinator, the crew would return to the destroyer for refueling in what would soon be called HIFR (high inflight refueling). The hoist operator would lower the hoist with a cloth bag to the deck. The destroyer crew would then take the bag off the hoist, attach a fueling nozzle to the hoist and give the Helo hoist operator the motion to lift. The hoist would raise the nozzle to the height of the Helo cargo door, while the second crew member would reach out and connect the nozzle to the fuel intake port, flip the handle to receive fuel, and wait for the shutoff and disconnect order. When finished, the hoist operator would lower the nozzle back to the destroyer's deck. The cloth bag, fresh from the galley and holding sandwiches, would be reattached, and raised to the crew above.

This so-called HIFR would extend the flight time of the H-3 from its normal four ½ hour to a much longer sojourn. Ron Clarke once logged a total of thirteen ½ hours in one flight. Normally at 13:00 hours a second SAR aircraft would be launched to relieve the morning flight. The armored seats of the pilots added protection, but not comfort.

The weather varied with the season, from periods of dryness to the monsoon season and with-it flight requirements varied from VFR to IFR. Outside, the air temperature normally hovered around 100 degrees and the long metal tube functioned as a convection oven for those inside. The crew members in the back had it a little better than the pilots. They had the luxury of airflow through the gun areas, whereas the pilots were surrounded by plexiglass in a greenhouse arrangement.

Normally a SAR detachment would only remain on any carrier for a week or two at a time, before transitioning to another carrier, complete with all tools, spare parts, personal gear etc. When they assumed the duties from HS 4, the Yorktown left Yankee Station and headed towards home, while the detachment transferred to the USS Constellation. When HS 4 departed, all the combat experience they had gained left with them. The only thing left for Det Alpha was to use the experiences that had been verbally transferred and pass those lessons along to the entire squadron.

A few days after assuming SAR duty, an A-4 from Attack Squadron 155 was attacking North Vietnamese patrol boats 15 miles east of Cat Ba, one of the seaward islands of the Fai Tsi Long Archipelago, when the plane was struck, forcing the pilot, Lieutenant Neil Holben to eject. When his chute hit the water, he found himself just 800 yards from one of the countless small but well defended islands.

On North SAR duty that day was the crew of CDR Warren Lockwood with LT. (jg) Ollie Donelson serving as copilot, AX1 Tom Goen as first crew member and ADJ1 Vic Vicari as second crew. For Vicari, this was his third war. He first served as a turret gunner in torpedo planes in WW2, flew as a crew member in Korea, and was now enjoying nearing retirement in sunny Vietnam.

The crew was vectored to the area, where an Air Force HU16 was already on station. The HU 16 located Lt. Holben in the water, dropped a smoke flare to mark his location, and exited afterwards as the enemy fire threatened to bring down the lumbering amphibian aircraft.

Lockwood's crew had followed the HU 16 into the area, and locating Holben, saw that the A-4 pilot was drawing fire from automatic weapons and mortar fire from the nearby islands. Holben had not abandoned his survival raft as the book instructed. As a result, Lockwood quickly assessed that Holben would be difficult to rescue by hoist as the rotor wash from his helicopter would cause the raft to move away from the path of the rescue craft. However, the Sea King Helo he was flying had a boat hull; one that, according to the sales pamphlet, could land and float when needed. Deciding this was its time of need, Cdr. Lockwood expertly landed on rough, choppy seas hellbent on getting Holben into the aircraft and returning him to the safety of the Constellation.

The rotors were kept steady to keep the top-heavy H-3 stable. However, none of them were ready for what happened next. Suddenly, the choppy sea tossed Holben's raft into the helo, throwing the downed pilot into water. Without a second's thought, Goen leaped after the pilot and soon had the rescue hoist connected to the now very wet Holben. With the pilot secured, Vicari quickly hit the hoist button, bringing Holben into the cabin.

It was a remarkable victory given the circumstances, but before any of the crew could launch into a celebration, they were hit by another misfortune.

Goen was caught in the downdraft and was blown behind the floating aircraft and out of sight. The combination of the downdraft and choppy sea made getting back to the floating craft more difficult. So, Vicari decided to communicate the new difficulties to the flight station. But it was at this moment that the interior communications of the aft cabin decided to quit. Without a moment's hesitation, he sped to the forward area and verbally passed his difficulties across to Ollie

Donelson. Donelson relayed the information to Lockwood, who at once took off and circled the aircraft, looking for the lost crew member. Fortunately, the pilots spotted Goen and entered a ten-foot hover, allowing Vicari to lower the hoist and bring Goen to safety.

Still under fire, the crew with the elated Holben aboard quickly left the area, making the flight the squadrons second successful rescue. Later, Donelson and Vicari were awarded Air Medals for valor, Lockwood, a Distinguished Flying Cross, and Goen the Silver Star.

***

A few days later Ron Clarke's crew was at the North SAR station and had just completed its third inflight HIFR refueling. The air temperature outside hovered near the 104-degree mark. The greenhouse effect of the flight station coupled with the hot Nomex flight suits, the flight vest, and the Mae West life preservers, made this one miserable day.

Clarke had flown with Air America in Laos a few years earlier and had learned that having at least cursory flight instruction for the gunners could be lifesaving. Today, ADJ3 George Armstrong was temporarily in co-pilot Jerry Smith's seat as Smith took the opportunity to stretch his legs and walk around the aft cabin.

Suddenly, the guard channel of 243 MHz began alerting friendly forces that one of the attacking aircraft was hit and was trying to make it to the Gulf of Tonkin before ejecting. Smith quickly regained his seat, and Clarke headed towards Haiphong Harbor.

They arrived in time to see the crippled Skyhawk in a final plunge to earth. The crew, alert to the dangers in the heavily defended area, picked up the sight of a parachute floating to the surface of the sea. Unfortunately, the downed pilot was floating near a small fleet of junks that were changing course to facilitate his capture. Clarke radioed overhead American jets requesting fire suppression but was told they were out of ordinance. Undeterred, Clarke decided to rescue the pilot himself. But to do that, he knew his crew would need to act at once. The H-3s carried sets of Sir Galahads: armor plating designed to be worn by the sitting pilots. Smith put his on, but Clarke learned the aircraft was one set short, and had to go in without armor plating.

The downed airman's flight, although out of ordinance, made attack runs on the junks to draw their attention. It was working for the time being, but Clarke knew that the junks would call their bluff soon when they realized the attacking jets were quite harmless.

Smith was at the controls, and he flew low enough to allow the hoist operators drop the rescue hoist in the water to ground any residual static electricity in the helo. When he pulled the cyclic back hard upon entering the hover, he found that his "Sir Galahad" armored chest plate was interfering with his range of cyclic control. When he would pull back on the cyclic his range of motion was hampered by the heavy armor plating of the Sir Galahad. He told Clarke he was having trouble holding hover, and the experienced pilot took control, pushing the cyclic forward as he turned left, and came around and re-entered the hover. In the meantime, Smith discarded the armor plate and retook control.

Without the "chicken plate" interfering, he had no further issues.

As soon as Jimmy Conrad, who was working the hoist, informed the flight station the downed pilot was in the sling and on the way up, Clarke rolled the nose forward with an emphatic, "Let's get the hell out of here." Immediately, Armstrong hauled the downed aviator into the cabin and the helo hastened out of the harbor, an A-4 tucked on each side for protection.

Safe on deck, the pilot, Bill Isenhour, moved to the flight station and greeted Clarke with, "You, helo jockeys are alright." He was informed they were flying him to the Piraz (Positive Radar Area Zone) destroyer in the area so the ships doctor could give him a medical examination, and he objected forcefully. He explained that this was the last combat strike of his squadron (Attack Squadron 216), who would be returning on the USS Hancock to the States that evening, and he would like to return with them. Clarke agreed and changed course to the Hancock. Isenhour and his newly found friends in the helo were soon greeted on the flight deck of the USS Hancock.

Thus, the first week of SAR duty finished with positive results. The courage and commitment of the pilots and crew of HS 6 had helped them tackle all early challenges. However, tougher missions were ahead of them.

Sar Det Alpha celebrates success. Rick Grant cuts the cake with Lcdr Nichols (L), Cdr. Lockwood (R) Lt. Waechter next to Lockwood. Wildman Center Petrovich between Grant and Wildman Photo courtesy Raunchy Redskins Ken Burns

Notes:
Clarke, R. *History of Sar Det Alpha*, Raunchy Redskins Web Site, Ken Burns
Badger, T, 2017, *The Saga of HS-6*
Galdorisi, G. & Phillips, T. (2008) *Leave No Man Behind,* Zenith Press
Raunchy Redskin site kept by Ken Burns
Operations, Combat SAR

CHAPTER 3

SAR DET ALPHA KEEPS ROLLING

Days after Ron Clarke and his crew pulled Isenhour from the drink, Bill Waechter was on the North SAR station. Flying as co-pilot was Bob Wildman with the crew of ADJ 2 Harley Olsen and AX 3 Michael Brantley.

Meanwhile, a flight of F-8 Crusaders from the Oriskany were buzzing the Kep Airfield, challenging the Migs to come up and fight. The airfield, thirty miles from Hanoi, held components of the Vietnamese Peoples Air Force.

To entice their opponents, the Americans began to perform touch and go maneuvers on the Kep Airfield. Still the Migs kept to the ground. Soon, the anti-aircraft batteries surrounding the runways began to fire furiously at the VF 162 pilots, finally hitting Lt. (jg) Rick Adams, who was forced to eject in the deep jungle area beyond the runway.

Waechter, hearing the Mayday call, obtained clearance from Red Crown control to make the rescue attempt, and headed inland at 2500 feet to avoid small arms fire. They went "feet dry" just north of Haiphong and soon came under fire by batteries of 100mm anti-aircraft units. The flak bursts were approaching Waechter's Big Mother aircraft but suddenly dissipated after being jammed by an electronic warfare plane.

Waechter gave permission to his gunners, Olsen, and Brantley, to return fire, and they complied, hosing any area that was throwing up tracers. Olsen saw a gun enclosure just ahead of the helicopter's path and promptly gave it quick bursts of well-aimed fire, scattering the NVA gunners.

A flight of four A-1 propeller aircraft flew as RESCAP (rescue combat air patrol) with a call sign of Locket. The Flight Leader, Lcdr. Eric Shade radioed that the helo was taking heavy fire, but Waechter and his 4 mother hens were not deterred and continued towards Adams.

Wildman could see Adams flight as they circled the field, attacking any enemy they spotted with their 20mm cannons; however, he still did not have a visual on Adams. Quickly, he contacted the aviator on his URC 10 survival radio, and he reported the same problem. He could hear the rotor blades but could not find his rescuers due to the heavy cover from the forest.

Finally, his parachute was spotted among the trees, and moments later he was seen. He had landed in a heavily forested area that was on a steep incline. Realizing that landing was out of the question and the 100 feet of cable the hoist supplied would not be enough, Waechter decided to descend into the jungled abyss.

With Wildman on the gauges and the gunners watching the rotor tips and their proximity to the jungle, he slowly lowered the collective and began the treacherous descent. Waechter soon realized he was shielded from all wind and the subsequent incidental lift it would provide; that, coupled with the heavy weight of the armor-plated bird, made it difficult to maintain 100% rotor rpm. Wildman pushed both engine controls to full power, but as Waechter continued to try and keep altitude the rotor rpm slowly decreased.

Waechter had a tough decision; he could allow the aircraft to slowly descend into the brush and keep his heading or allow the helo to rotate around its axis and divert the power from the tail rotor to the main rotor. The Big Mother bird slowly started spinning to the right as Waechter tried to move the tail rotor toward the left. He put as much strength as he could muster into controlling the spin, but even full left rudder was not enough to halt the spin as the helo slowly descended.

Olsen, having lowered the hoist and the jungle penetrator, pleaded with Waechter to stop the rotation, but Waechter told him he had to make do with a tough situation as he could not stop the spin. Once Olsen saw Adams, he deployed the seat hooks of the penetrator, and started hauling him up to the cabin, trying to avoid outstretched branches along the way. At this point, the aircraft was rotating at a rate of a full turn in two minutes.

As soon as Olsen told Waechter that Adams was on his way up, the pilot pushed the cyclic slightly forward, increasing the turn rate, which in turn raised the rotor rpm. Finally, he was able to depart from the Karst-formed depression and into forward flight, regaining control of the aircraft.

Having egressed the dense forest, the Big Mother crew sped towards the relative safety of the coast, reacquainting themselves with the flak batteries that continued to throw salvo after salvo their way. The armor-plated bird vibrated intensely under the strain; something the crew was familiar with, but a wide-eyed Adams found to be a new experience. He was soon back with his squadron on the Oriskany.

Waechter would receive a Silver Star for his efforts, Wildman the Distinguished Flying Cross, and the gunners were awarded the Air Medal for Valor.

Three days later, the 15th of July, a flight of Air Force F 105's was north of Haiphong when their leader, Capt. Carl Hamby was lost while attacking a transportation area.

He maintained flight until clearing the coast and promptly called Mayday after he was feet wet. He described it this way, ""When you wake up in the morning with a sinking feeling, just hope you are not leading a flight of 4 F-105s to route number 6 in North Vietnam. White flight in the 34th TFS had only 4 pilots and Ken Blank was on R&R in Bangkok, so Bob Reed filled-in the 4th slot. We did not have a spare. After start-up, Tom Curtis, the element leader called to say his airplane was not quite ready. I was Lead, Dave Groark was two, and Bob Reed was four, so we taxied and took off on time. After passing Ubon, Tom Curtis called that he was airborne, and he joined up as we orbited at the Mekong River. We met the tanker over the Gulf, one and two refueled with no problem, but Tom got a couple of disconnects, then Reed got several before he finished refueling. Since we had a 650-gallon centerline and two 3,000 lbs. bombs, I decided to depart the tanker on time. There were low clouds starting at the coast with a 3,000-foot ceiling, so we flew in at about 2,500 feet. We did not know that the

Weasel Flight and Fred Tracy's Flight went in above a 10,000-foot cloud cover, which was against our Squadron Policy in SAM country. There was no flak until we approached the NE Railroad where both the Weasels and Tracy were in orbit at 12,000 feet. The sky was black with flak but gunners didn't know that the 57mm range was just short of that. I was not happy at all with this situation and called to take it up above their altitude for a left roll in to bomb the railroad, which I did and started a pull up recovery doing 1.3 mach. Then I started/continued doing things we never did, such as slowing down for the rejoin, 2,3 and 4 came off the bomb run okay, but when I slowed below 500 kts, they passed me like I was going the other way and they went between the clouds. I pushed the throttle up only to encounter a thunderstorm, when that super cold water hit that super-heated engine—you guessed it—she blew up, smoke in the cockpit, all the red lights on, but I was climbing, I jettisoned the canopy and was coasting out, she was on fire but traveling much faster than I could walk.

At about 15,000 feet and 20 miles south of Haiphong, I lost control and bailed out. The airplane was 65 feet of flame in a circling descent when it hit the water. After I was in the water, I lit an orange flare that brought the helicopter to my rescue, then to the carrier Ranger. Gordy Williams was standing on the deck smiling when he saw me—what a grand sight that was. He had been high cap in F4s. The COD took me to Danang the next day and after a rain-soaked night in a tent, I paid my BOQ fees and went to the Command Post, rang the buzzer, and out came a friend I had known at Luke AFB who typed me some orders to ride a C-130 to Korat.…While on the Ranger, I learned that four A4s were lost on the first mission that day and they had four more missions to fly that day—made me even more glad to be flying F-105s from Korat in the Air Force."

When the HS 6 crew was egressing the area, co-pilot Ollie Donelson, believed he saw ground fire coming from the lighthouse on Grand Norway Island. That info was relayed to the RESACP and scratch one lighthouse.

Later Donelson would quip, the fire from the lighthouse may have been due to one nervous JG (himself). The 1963 graduate of the Naval Academy would distinguish himself many times during his time with HS 6.

Later that month, on the 24th of July, Lt. E.L. Foss from Attack Squadron 55 was hit while over the North Vietnamese mainland. The South Sar Station was being manned by the crew of Lcdr Ron Nichols, co-pilot Lt (jg) Rick Grant and crew of AX-3 Gary Smith and AMH-2 Royce Roberts. At 17:51 the crew heard Foss call Mayday and with an ADF cut on Foss's transmission immediately headed at high speed towards Foss. Two minutes later the South Sar ship, the USS Reeves have Nichols crew a vector of 217 degrees and 36 miles.

When the helo, was five miles from the downed pilot, the flight crew spotted his smoke. When they had closed to within a mile, a RESCAP aircraft joined them. They were only a few miles distance from the Cap Mui Ron Peninsula, and well within the range of the anti-aircraft artillery at that location. Big

Mother 51 made a high-speed approach using evasive tactics to thwart the NVA defenders. It made a sharp 180 degree turn when reaching the survivor, placing their tail towards the enemy guns. The rescue went without a hitch and the hover was only thirty seconds in duration. Nichols and crew delivered their wet prize directly to the USS Ranger after the gunners had determined that he did not require immediate medical attention.

Notes:
HS-6 Raunchy Redskin site Ken Burns webmaster
Carl Hamby 34th TFS Thuds History web search
Lcdr Nichols after action report, HS-6 Raunchy Redskin site

CHAPTER 4

RON CLARKE'S WILD RIDE

In the early morning of July 27, 1966, Ron Clarke and his co-pilot Jerry Smith were having breakfast in the wardroom of the USS Ranger when he was called to the phone. The Combat Information Center (CIC) was following an event that had been developing near the DMZ.

Stiletto One, a reconnaissance F-4, with the 16th Tactical Reconnaissance Squadron, flying out of Ton Son Nhut Air Base in Saigon, (now Ho Chi Minh City), had been hit and lost on a low-level approach. The pilot, who had only been in Vietnam for two weeks was on his first night mission. Captain Mayfield and his back seater had made four runs over the area, dropping flares that activated the night cameras. On the fifth pass, Mayfield recalled that he felt a rumble, like when a car runs over a rock at 60 mph. He wrote to his daughter Lori, "…almost at once stability augmentation-like power steering on a car was lost. Within a half second, I lost all instrument lights and the plane inverted. Both engines flamed out. I was thrown upward against the canopy. My only ground reference was the anti-aircraft artillery fire still shooting at me. I tried to eject with the primary handle above my head, but my helmet prevented it from being pulled far enough to activate the system. We were getting close to the ground, so I made a fast grab for the alternate ejection handle beneath the seat…it worked at a rapid rate." The Martin Baker ejection system automatically opens the canopy of the airplane and blasts the seat with small rocket motors. "I separated from the plane and the chute opened immediately," he told his daughter. He later told Lt. Clarke that his chute only swung two times before he hit the ground hard. He had the breath knocked from him and was bleeding from the nose and mouth. He had bitten off part of his tongue.

"My back hurt (broken tail bone) and my ankle was obviously sprained. Within a few moments I got up and started walking.

I fell several times but got up and kept moving."

Cleverly, he waded across a rice paddy and concealed himself in a hedge row. As he regained his senses slowly, he remembered his survival radio. He tried it repeatedly but only heard bull frogs in the distance as a reply. He kept trying and finally connected with a Marine pilot. The Marine alerted other forces and three B57 Canberra's were soon on the scene.

The Marine pilots' calls were soon picked up by CIC in the Ranger and Clarke was alerted. No sooner had he been alerted by the officer on duty in CIC than he asked to have his helo spotted for take-off and to send a runner to alert his crew members, Armstrong, and Conrad.

The Air Force, in 1966 did not make night rescue attempts However, the Navy pilots trained in ASW were used to nighttime hovers and the SH-3A's doppler altimeter would be a major asset on a dark night—and that night was very dark. As if that was not enough, there was also the added visual impairment of heavy rains, making it impossible for Clarke and Smith to make out the water beneath them. He called the B-57s on the scene and was asked if he wanted the IP (initial point of entry) marked. Clarke replied in the affirmative and moments later a huge explosion illuminated the beach as the B-57s dropped a bomb near the water's edge. For the first time, Clarke was able to distinguish the terrain below them.

He then keyed his radio, "Stiletto One, this is Indian Gal, do you copy, over." Mayfield replied he did. "Give me a short count." Mayfield turned his survival radio selector to warble and keyed the mike; using this function would prevent enemy soldiers in the area from hearing his voice. Having received the warbling signal, Clarke looked at his gauges and the automatic direction finder found the signal and gave him a line of bearing. Then he turned his aircraft into the direction shown on the ADF.

Clarke knew this area was very heavily defended with the possibility of SAM (surface to air) sites being situated there as well. He knew that SAM sites were manned by a fire control system NATO called Fansong and that it had a minimum discrimination altitude of 500 feet. Flying below that would aid against surface to air missiles but also make them fair game for ground fire. Clarke decided to risk the SAM's and ingresses at 3200 feet.

Peering forward, Smith warned, "Here it comes." In front of the helicopter was a field of solid crisscrossing tracers. Captain Mayfield later recalled, "From the instance he came into view, the ground fire started." He now was aware of the desperate situation ahead. It was a low moment in his morale, "I could see I was surrounded."

The helo crew would later recall how intense that moment was. Large anti-aircraft shells, many of 57mm variety, threw huge fireballs in their path, while B40 handheld rockets (RPG 2) took potshots at the crew.

Clarke took evasive action, unexpectedly throwing Conrad in the aft cabin out of the aircraft. Prior to the mishap, Conrad had worn his gunners' belt, made from heavy duty nylon and leather, and fastened it securely around his waist prepared for an occasion like this. He found himself hanging from the left side of the cabin two feet under the door but was also presented with a gift—an excellent view of the enemy fire both in front and behind him. Conrad thought it looked like flaming softballs rising from the darkness below and crossing the path of their aircraft.

As Conrad pulled himself aboard, Clarke called out to the bombers for support. They began dropping 1,000-pound ordinance on either side of Clarke's crew. The crew watched as napalm engulfed a hut in a rice paddy. Prior to this attack, the hut had been seen as a source of tracer fire. But that problem was alleviated after the fire ball consumed the area.

When Clarke noticed heavy fire, "Huge fireballs," coming from his 11 o'clock position, he reached out to one of the Air Force bombers, who nullified that area with ordinance.

Mayfield watched as the ordinance moved quantities of earth, hurtling them skyward. He had said later, "No one could have blamed the crew if they would have done a 180 degree turn and got out of there, least of all me."

For 27 continuous minutes, the crew braved this fire, while Armstrong and Conrad heated barrel after barrel as they expended thousands of rounds of 7.62mm ammo in defense of their mission. In the darkness, the gunners could see their barrels change color, moving from a dark grey to a warming red. As the barrel heated, its accuracy fell off. The gunner would unlatch the used barrel and toss it aside to cool as he loaded a spare barrel and continued suppression fire.

Clarke asked Stiletto One for another short count and his ADF swung 180 degrees, proving he had overflown the position. Ahead, at a two o'clock low position, Clarke saw a beam of light pointing skyward. "Stiletto One, do you have a flashlight on?" "Yes," came the reply.

"Turn it off!" Mayfield pointed the light downward before turning it off.

"I've got you," Clarke said as he dropped his collective control and descended rapidly. He maneuvered towards the area where he believed he had last seen the light. Then he flared and landed where he thought the downed pilot was hiding. As if on cue, he looked in his mirror and saw what he thought was a person leaping a hedge row. Immediately, he called to Smith, "Full power!"

He caught a man leaping into the cargo area in the mirror and lifted his collective. Keeping the nose low, he accelerated away from the area. When Mayfield leapt into the cabin, he slid along the thousands of empty shell casings across the floor and into the troop seat area.

Then Armstrong, a Blackfoot Native American from Idaho, exclaimed, "Here they come, let's get out of here!" He could see a myriad of enemy fighters coming into view. This, in the opinion of the gunners, was the crew from the AAA site in that area. His warrior ancestry would have been proud to see this unflappable crew member open fire on his tormentors. Though his gun jammed moments later, he was quick to clear the jam with his survival knife. Later, when they were safe on the carrier, he would discover that in the heat of battle, with adrenaline flowing like rainwater, he had sliced his hand open several times. But his reaction would be stoic and comedic: "Boys, in the old days, mom would have taken my scalping knife from me, for fear I would hurt myself."

The anti-aircraft fire recommenced as the helo began its sojourn to the coast. It had been 27 minutes of steady fire coming in and it was 27 minutes of tracers leaving the DMZ. Remarkably, the crew withdrew without suffering casualties.

When Mayfield asked Conrad when the crew would go back across the beach for his back seater, he was told it would have to wait until he was safely aboard the USS Ranger. While he was still in the air, Clarke heard that an Air Force Jolly Green was headed into the area they had just vacated. Quickly, he recommended getting fighter cover to suppress the groundfire, but the Jolly chose to ignore his advice, and continue its mission to rescue his compatriot. Soon after, the Jolly communicated through radio that he had been hit, suffered severe damage, and needed to withdraw.

Later in the day, the crew learned that the photo officer had been rescued by a Jolly Green that snuck in from Laos after attack planes had softened the area with bombs and rockets.

Mayfield, in his report said simply, "Thank God for the Navy, as our Air Force helicopters are not allowed night operations." The actual flight was 2 ½ hours in total.

The two crew members had expended over 3,000 rounds of their ammunition. They had to change barrels many times and clear countless jams as their guns began to foul.

Conrad later wrote of the deficiencies that the ASW crews and aircraft were experiencing. He thought the H-3 was "too large, too slow, too vulnerable, and much too loud." He pointed out that this aircraft was designed to hover over water and use its dipping sonar to find Russian submarines, and, except for insignificant amounts of armor plating, self-sealing tanks etc., it was still not the best platform. Conrad went on to say that apart from Ron Clarke, no one in the helicopter had any SAR training. He and Armstrong had but 30 minutes training with the M60, a weapon he had found wanting. At an altitude of 3,000 feet, the muzzle velocity was not high enough to be considered a threat. In live fire practice in the Gulf, he and Armstrong decided their best chance of fire suppression was to have tracer ammunition linked at a higher rate than the 1:7 in the tins (actual linkage was 1:5 as mandated by the Geneva Accords). He believed that the greater concentration of tracers in his feed helped suppress the fire they experienced.

Crew receiving awards. Photo from the Kearsarge cruise book 1966. Caption misidentifies Armstrong as ADJ3 Thompson. Also credits incorrectly the two gunners as receiving DFC vice Air Medals

Lt. Clarke was awarded the Silver Star for Conspicuous Gallantry, although later attempts to upgrade the award to the Medal of

Honor were not successful for the lack of living eyewitnesses to the event. LT (jg) Smith received the Distinguished Flying Cross George Armstrong and Jimmy Conrad both were awarded Air Medals for valor

Notes:
Recollections from Jimmy Conrad DVM
Recollections of Ronald E Clarke
Conversations with George Armstrong 2017
Mayfield, L. (2003) *Rescuing My Father*
Galdorisi, G. & Phillips, T. (2008) *Leave No Man Behind,* Zenith Press
Risher, R. 2022 Wings of Gold "Indian Summer"

CHAPTER 5

FAI TSI LONG AGAIN

On August 11, 1966, Lcdr. Ron Nichols, Lt. (jg) Rick Grant, AMH2 Royce Roberts and AX3 Gary Smith were vectored to the Fai Tsi Long Archipelago again. They had made a rescue the previous month on the same string of islands. On this day, they approached the southern string of islands searching for a downed F-8 Crusader jockey, Lt. (jg) C.A. Balesteri. Balesteri had been commissioned in 1964 and was on his first deployment with Fighting 111 aboard the USS Oriskany.

Nichols approached the area using low altitude evasive maneuvers to thwart the known NVA artillery positions. This area was known to have both 85mm and 100mm defenses. Then Grant spotted a flare that Balesteri had deployed. He was on the Isle des L'Union, beneath a 400-foot cliff that would exceed the rescue hoist and keep its 100-feet of cable from reaching him.

Having discarded his raft and Mae West, Balesteri was not at ease to swim to a point where the crew could hoist him aboard.

So, Smith leaped into the water with an inflatable raft and moved to the beach where Balesteri was found. Then used the raft as support as they swam to a point where the helo could hoist them aboard.

Sometimes fate has a cruel sense of humor for it was at this moment the hoist failed, making Roberts unable to lower the cable; this forced them to devise an alternative plan immediately. Nichols hovered near the water, with Grant on the gauges and power controls and they nimbly approached the stranded duo. Using the boat hull of the Sea King to his advantage, Nichols taxied to the raft with the aid of Roberts and Grant. Then Robert proceeded to pull both men into the aircraft.

At once, Nichols added collective power, nosed the helo over to gain speed, and left the scene with the fighter pilot onboard. He then used evasive actions to avoid NVA interdictory fire as they left the area.

Rick Grant, Harley Olsen, Royce Roberts, Gary Smith, Ron Nichols Photo courtesy Raunchy Redskins Ken Burns

Sadly, Balesteri would lose his life shortly after the event in the conflagration that hit the Oriskany. That will be covered in a later chapter along with the contributions of HS 6 to saving lives and aiding the carrier.

For their actions that day, Nichols would receive the Distinguished Flying Cross. Grant, Smith, and Roberts would be awarded the Air Medal for valor.

The following day when the USS Kearsarge arrived in Yankee Station, the detachment reunited with the squadron. In the past few weeks SAR Det Alpha had flown from the Yorktown, Ranger, Constellation, and the Intrepid; they had flown from the Constellation on two separate occasions. Now they were with the rest of their squadron, they would waste no time transferring their hard-won knowledge to the other crews.

* * *

On the 13th, Grant found himself in familiar waters again; this time flying with Lcdr George Tarrico with AX3 Gary Smith and ATR2 Arnie Hardin as crew.

F8 Crusader jockey, Lcdr Norman Levy had been hit by anti-aircraft fire but was able to stay with the plane and eject safely in the Fai Tsi area. While Grant and Smith possessed relative experience about the area as they had rescued Balesteri nearby just two days prior, it was new to Lcdr Tarrico and Hardin. Regardless, the rescue was unopposed and was performed without incident. Levy would be returned to his squadron, VF 111, and the Oriskany. He would also be a victim of the Oriskany fire.

* * *

One week later, on the 20th of August, Lt. Bill Roy, Lt. Vann Goodloe, and a crew of

AX3 Roger Sitko and AX3 Russell Sprague were on a logistics mission, delivering much-wanted mail and other supplies to the outlying ships of Task Force 77. They were also on an HS squadrons primary duty, ASW training. For this training, the search and rescue helos had their dipping sonar removed and an aluminum plate covering the hole where the transducer and cable reel once sat. These missions in the Gulf were a respite from what the SAR crews had been experiencing.

However, things would get serious in a hurry.

Roy got the call that his crew was needed north of the city of Dong Hoi as an Air Force Reconnaissance F-4C had been lost early that morning. The pilot, Captain Tiff Hawks had landed in a thicket, and had gathered the chute, helmet, seat survival kit, and hid them in the undergrowth.

Then he began to push through the thickets, encountering very little resistance. He could hear animals all around him, reinforced by the sound of the enemy hot on his trail. His survival school training kicked in, until he found a path through the dense brush. Given that he wanted to get as far as possible from the crash site, he ignored one of the most popular advice in survival school, "Stay off the paths." Soon, he found himself constantly stumbling and slipping on a clay path. He became in dire need of jungle boots and the sturdy soles they provided. However, when the night started to fade and the path became lit by the dawn, his journey grew easier. But he could still hear his pursuers. He thought he heard at least three dogs barking and a gong pealing among those hunting him.

In the stress of the moment, Hawks had forgotten his call sign, and began to rack his brain for it. At first, he thought the word tornado was close, and quite auspiciously, later remembered it was torpedo. When he heard planes overhead, he immediately called out, "Aircraft overhead this is Torpedo."

He was relieved to hear, "Roger, we have your position. We will get someone into you right away."

However, as he saw the NVA forces start closing in on his position, Hawks became apprehensive that his rescuers would not arrive in time. He had lost his sidearm earlier and was totally unarmed except for his survival knife. He relayed to Locket (call sign on the A1 plane overhead) that the enemy was advancing on his position from the SE of the mountain and was but 200 feet away. Then he asked for Locket to strafe their positions. In return, Locket received AAA fire from the south of the mountain and automatic weapons fire from SE of the knoll Hawks was occupying. Time was indeed running out for Hawks.

Rescue command knew they needed an armored bird, but it was more than an hour away. So, Roy's unarmored bird would need to suffice as command had decided there would not be time to call for an Air Force Jolly Green or an armored USN Big Mother. Roy accepted the task without hesitation even though he knew he lacked both armor and armament. When the enemy began throwing green tracers his way, Sprague and

Sisko could only cast spitballs or a thermos of left-over morning coffee in return.

The leader of the flight of A-1s from VA-152 was the on-scene commander, Lt. John Feldhaus. Aided by a flare that Hawks had thrown into the clearing, the helo sped to the site. Roy expertly guided his craft towards Hawks as he saw enemy troops closing in to within a fraction of a football field's distance from the downed pilot.

When Roy was five minutes from the ridge, Locket flight made constant strafing attacks from NW to SE of the ridge. Hawks related, "As the chopper approached, I ran down and around the north side of the little knoll to the chopper. There was automatic weapons fire all around me. I grabbed the jungle penetrator, unfolded the seat, threw my legs around it, and put the harness around my body, to prevent me from falling in case I was shot on the way up. They hoisted me up, taking off as before I was in the cabin, they were unarmored and received intense automatic weapons fire."

Roy's crew exited without further incident, flying Hawks to the carrier to be transported to his base. For his efforts that day, Lt. Roy received the Silver Star for conspicuous gallantry, Lt. Goodloe the Distinguished Flying Cross, and Sprague and Sitko the Air Medal for valor.

Roy's crew L-R Goodloe, Roy, Sprague, Sitko. Island of the USS Kearsarge in background

Notes:
Carl Hamby 34th TFS Thuds History web search
PACAF Evasion and Recovery Report, Hawks, Edwin T, Captain USAF, web search
Raunchy Redskin Site (HS-6) courtesy of Ken Burns
Galdorisi, G. & Phillips, T. (2008) *Leave No Man Behind*, Zenith Press

CHAPTER 6

CONTINUED SUCCESS

On August 21st, Captain Norman Wells, a pilot with the 354th Tactical Fighter Squadron Operating out of the Royal Thai Air Base at Takhli was on his 75th mission when he got hit by enemy AAA fire over Kep Airfield. His F-105 Thud held together long enough for him to reach the Gulf of Tonkin, where he was rescued by an unidentified HS 6 crew.

Captain Wells was returned to his squadron, only to be shot down a second time on the 29th of August. He was captured and would spend 2379 days (about 6 and a half years) in captivity. Earlier in July he had been credited with a MIG kill, that would eventually lead to his being awarded the Air Force Cross.

On the 27th of August HS 6 commanding officer, Cdr. Bob Vermilya, Lt. (jg) Vern von Sydow, AXC Tom Grisham and AX3 Roger Sitko were taking part in an ASW night training exercise when a Mayday call changed their mission. The pilots vectored their unarmored SH-3A to an area 3 miles from the enemy coastline. The pilot and back seater were flying an F4C Phantom from the 497th Tactical Fighter Squadron. The squadron flew its missions from Ubon, Thailand.

Also on this training exercise was the crew of Lcdr. David Humphrey, Lt. (jg) Dick Lynas, AX3 Dave Hannum, and AX1 Kenneth White. They were also vectored to the same area.

The two Air Force flyers, Maj. J.E. Barrow, and 1st Lt. T.H. Walsh, parachuted safely, landing within the same vicinity, and were rescued by the two HS 6 crews. However, the specifics of which crew rescued which downed flyer was not recorded for posterity.

On the 29th of August, Lt. Bill Roy and HS-6 flight surgeon Lt. Bob Stemsrud air evacuated the two downed fliers to the hospital in Danang. As they touched down on the hospital's landing pad, their unarmored SH-3A was struck by ground fire, rupturing the fuel cell. Regardless of that, Roy soldiered on, landing the helo safely, and no injuries occurred.

On the 31st of August, Skipper Vermilya flying with Ens. Bill Runyon as co-pilot and AXC Grisham, ADR2 Jerry Dunford as crew were vectored to the Haiphong area after a Mayday was issued by a reconnaissance pilot trying to photograph foreign tankers in the harbor. Flying with Vermilya was the photographer's Mate 2nd Class Mike Delamore trying to gain useful photos for the Kearsaga, the magazine produced by the crew of the USS Kearsarge. His photos highlighted the mission.

Haiphong was heavily fortified as it was the major port for receiving war supplies for the North Vietnamese. Flying into the harbor would be a major undertaking for a low and slow helicopter, but when in the rescue business, one must go to where the customers can be found, hence the motto, "You fall, we haul. Call 243 MHZ for service."

Lcdr. Tommy Tucker had been dealt a tough hand. His mission was to photograph the shipping in the harbor, and as the only plane making the run, all eyes and all guns would be on him.

To combat this difficulty, he decided to pilot his RF-8G from landward side to the ocean, hoping that if he were hit, at least, he would be heading towards the Tonkin Gulf and Task Force 77. He began his run, cameras on, eyes on altitude, and that was when he saw the awaiting flak bursts ahead: big stuff, consisting of the green tracers of the Soviet Made PPK heavy machine guns and the 37MM flak. It was a tough day to be a recon pilot. Tucker moved stick and rudder to avoid the steel curtain being erected near him, but he was hit, and almost immediately began to lose control.

He ejected at 1500 feet (about the height of the Empire State Building), and saw, floating to sea, he was still being fired on. He came to a wet landing near a Russian supply ship and docked. He could see the Russians lowering a lifeboat, and the Vietnamese sampans and small sailboats heading his way. Then he looked up and saw another F-8, flown by Lcdr. "Tooter" Teague make a strafing run and sending the craft back to shore.

Vermilya's crew had just HIFR refueled for the second time when they received their call to action. A RF-8G pilot had misplaced his aircraft and was now in need of a ride to the fleet. Vermilya was awaiting the SAR commander, Harbor Master's clearance to attempt the rescue and for RESCORT (Rescue Escort) planes to join up. Teague, seeing the situation below, pleaded, "If they do not hurry, they may as well save the trip."

Every time Teague switched channels, he momentarily lost communication with Tucker, causing uneasiness on the downed pilot who was now feeling very alone.

Vermilya flew in at 3,000 feet to mitigate ground fire. Six miles out, two surface to air missiles exploded, their five-hundred-pound warheads igniting the unburned rocket fuel in a pyrotechnical display that normally would have been enjoyed at home and on the fourth of July. However, the crew was nearing the North Vietnamese' primary shipping hub, and their appreciation for fireworks was diminished.

Vermilya decreased altitude until he was just feet above the waves. Then Teague assumed the role of RESCORT and cleared a path for Vermilya's aircraft, strafing anything he saw as a hinderance to the rescue crew.

Alone and awaiting rescue on his raft, Tucker heard the gunfire in the channel, which heralded the arrival of the Big Mother, and was instantly filled with hope. Meanwhile, the junks and shore batteries continued to fire on the onrushing helo. Tucker lit a smoke flare, only to watch, to his dismay, the helo pass over him. It turned out that with all the fire, Vermilya and Runyon were yet to spot the floating Tucker. Fortunately, Grisham saw the smoke out his port gun position and called the attention of the flight station.

Lcdr Tommy Tucker being hoisted aboard. USN photo. PH2 Delamore

Immediately, Vermilya banked hard and initiated a hover over the bobbing Tucker. Then the crew lowered the hoist and Tucker hooked himself on.

On his way up, Vermilya nosed the helo over, gaining speed, and started to make his getaway. Quickly, the photographer grabbed his camera and began to record the moment. He had hopped a lift, hoping to get a day in the life of a helo crew, and was being accommodated beyond his wildest wishes.

Still, they continued drawing fire from the nearby junks and sampans, and the two crew members returned fire.

After getting into the cabin, Tucker went to the cabin door and began to aid Chief Grisham in feeding the M60. He had been shot at while in his chute, while helpless in the water, and while being rescued. He was mad and he wanted payback. So, he pleaded for the helo to stick around a little longer and allow him to hose down his tormentors with 7.62mm revenge pills. Chief Grusham remembered discretion is a part of valor and withheld fire.

Afterwards, the helo crew took stock and examined their aircraft as they cleared the harbor. Grisham checked the cabin and pylon, while Dunford handled the forward section. Remarkably, after double checking, they realized they had not taken a hit. Tucker was incredulous; he had flown in the same area, at a much higher speed, and with a more maneuverable plane and he had been shot out of the sky. This seemed to him like a miracle. The Kearsarge photographer continued to take shots as the action unfolded. He would have a story to relate to the rest of the staff when he returned.

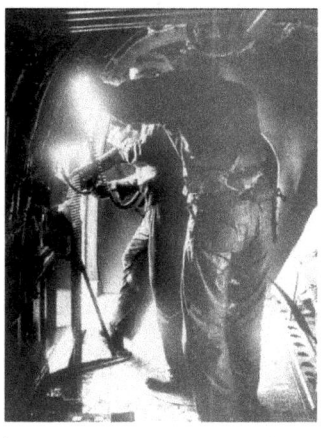

Tucker with Grisham at port gun mount. Tucker wanted payback for being shot at while in his parachute USN photo. PH2 Mike Delamore

August had closed out with a bang.

Cdr. Vermilya was awarded the Silver Star, Ens. Runyon the Distinguished Flying Cross, and the crew men the Air Medal for Valor. Delamore was rewarded with the most interesting pictures of his cruise and a hair-raising story to relate for all time.

In a few days' time, September 2, SAR Det Bravo would be transferred to the USS Intrepid as the Kearsarge leaves Yankee Station for a crew rest in Olongapo City.

On September 12, SAR Det Bravo would return to the Kearsarge as it returned to Yankee Station.

The following day, SAR Det Charlie assumed SAR duty.

On the 14th of September, the squadron crews were called again; this time with Lt. W.P. Mathews, Lcdr. Leon Houghlum, AX3 Don Stanford and AX3 Chester Wood flying in the North SAR Station. They were vectored deep inside the Fai Tsi Long system to rescue an Air Force Thud pilot from the 421st TFS.

On the scene, an Air Force Crab Crusher tried to close in on the downed pilot, 1st Lt, John Casper, but was driven off by heavy ground fire from the nearby islands. The RESCAP (Rescue Combat Air Patrol) then suppressed the fire with 4 20mm auto cannons and air to ground rockets, allowing Mathew's helo to have a better reception from the locals.

Matthews, originally from Ironton, Mo. told the Tribune Wire Services that they had been flying on station for two hours when they heard the Mayday and were cleared by Harbor Master to make the attempt. At first, Matthews and his RESCORT were on the wrong side of the island where the now very wet Casper was found. Once they circled the island and had a visual on the downed aviator, they quickly executed a hover. Though the hoist gave trouble, the hoist operator Stanford was able to fix it temporarily and bring Casper up. Bringing the downed aviator up through the hoist was not an easy one as Casper initially slipped from the horse collar designed to support him. This mishap was due to Casper's water-wing flotation device, which prevented him from seating firmly in the sling. However, once he freed himself from it, the rescue continued without further complications.

The RESCORT planes continued to work the nearby islands that were firing on the departing helo with automatic weapons, mortars, and small arms. Then Matthews guided the fleeing craft gingerly through the maze of islands with both gunners firing at the origins of any tracers coming their way. Finally, they were clear and out of range after being under fire for 34 minutes. HS 6's luck remained in place and another pilot had been snatched from death or capture.

On the 17th Lcdr Bob McCaffery and crew rescued an A4 pilot without incident. SAR Det Charlie was on board the Kearsarge. On the 2nd of October Lt. (jg) Gale Prickett and Lt. (jg) Dick Lynas and crew, while on a logistics flight, rescued AMH3 Harrison, a flight deck crew member on the USS Oriskany.

* * *

On October 9, Lcdr Charles Tanner, and Lt. Ross Terry of Fighter Squadron 154 launched from the USS Coral Sea and were operating south of Hanoi when they were shot down. Lt. Bob Burnand and his crew consisting of co-pilot, Lt. Russ Mordhorst and gunners Roy Powell and Royce Roberts were primed for the mission and set off as soon as the Harbor Master cleared Big Mother 66. Though the downed aviators had not been found, RESCAP would aid on the scene. The RESCAP comprised of two A1 propeller driven planes from the Intrepid piloted by members of Attack Squadron 176.

The three aircraft—one helo and two Korean War veteran RESCAP planes—soon came under fire from the AAA in the Phu Ly area, but it did not deter the search for the downed aviators, Tanner and Terry. To add to their discomfort, the NVA command had scrambled two MIG 17s. The MIG 17 was a supersonic fighter armed with two 23mm and one 37 mm autocannon. Although this plane was being replaced in the Soviet air regiments, it had success against American fighters due to its great maneuverability and heavy gun armament. By the time the hostilities were over, it had bagged a total of 28 victories including F-4s, F-8s, and F-105s.

The two RESCAP planes descended to tree top height, constantly maneuvering, and turning into the paths of the oncoming MIGS. Running for cover was not an option as they would be caught and flamed by the much faster MIGS and leaving the hapless helo with Burnard's crew was not an option. Help from fighter aircraft was also far from the scene.

However, at the dearth of fighter cover, another helo approached the area escorted by two more Skyraiders. These planes, with the affectionate nickname of Spads, were piloted by two pilots from the same VA 176 squadron, Lt. Pete Russell, and Lt. (jg) Tom Patton.

Later Patton, in an oral history interview, would laugh at the incoming cavalry composed of two Skyraiders and a helo, "that must have really made him comfortable.". Then he would continue to tell the tale of his arrival on the scene. "I could see a MIG shooting at our guys, it was from a few miles off, but I could see little puffs of smoke."

"I saw one start after me. He was down low, and I was higher so I decided I would try something I had done before playing around with other jets. I timed it so when he was approaching me, I started a split S maneuver and when I came out of it, I was doing somewhere around 380 knots. I ended up higher than him and behind him. I did not have a great shot but started firing at him anyway."

The MIG pilot pulled up, which Patton, expected and he jockeyed to remain on his tail. "I don't think he realized I was still on him because he stopped maneuvering. I was about 50 yards behind him and opened with my guns. They suddenly stopped and I realized I was out of ammo. I fired a Zuni, an air to ground weapon and of course it missed. We split S turned through the clouds and I followed and fired a second Zuni. I heard later heard stories that it hit him, but I know it missed also. I was now abeam of the MIG and suddenly I saw the pilot eject."

For that SAR mission, the loss of the MIG was their only victory. Dangerously low on fuel, and unable to contact the two Americans stranded on the ground , Burnand had no choice but to withdraw. His crew began to jettison all non-essential gear to lighten the load.

Pilots of Sar Det C. Oct 1966 Top L-R, Ross Mordhorst, Buck Carlton, Vern von Sydow, Bob Burnand, Doug Heggie, Vann Goodloe, Bill Roy, Ed Marsyla (in sling from wounds received on Shining Brass Mission Bottom row Tom May, Leon Houglum Bill Medley, and Dave Murphy photo courtesy HS 6 Raunchy Redskins, Ken Burns

Meanwhile, the USS Wiltsie, DD 716, a Gearing class destroyer whose keel had been laid during WW2 sped towards the shoreline. The Engineman, Don Adams, recalled his skipper announcing that they had a chopper inbound dangerously low on fuel and in danger of crashing. The Wiltsie proceeded so near the coast that the fish traps from the local villagers could be seen on either side of the destroyer. The 2500-ton ship normally drew 14½ feet of water and it was getting as close as possible.

The air support saw items fly from the helo as the fuel state got critical. Objects like ammo were sacrificed to get every inch of flight out of every drop of the precious fuel. As soon as the helo approached the fantail of the Wiltsie, Adams ran to the high drink station, quickly fastened the refueling hose to the hoist, and watched the nozzle and hose, hoping it would ascend to the helo cabin. The moment the nozzle and hose got there, the crew members attached the nozzle, opened the valve, and felt relieved. Swim call was canceled for the day.

Later, it was learned that Tanner and Terry were taken prisoner the moment their feet touched ground. They were not released until 1973.

On the 11th, SAR Det Charlie would be transferred to the USS Intrepid.

Notes:
Galdorisi, G. & Phillips, T. (2008) *Leave No Man Behind,* Zenith Press
Oral History Project: Tom Patton | "I saw a MiG coming at me." Former Intrepid crew

member and VA-176 Skyraider pilot William T. "Tom" Patton describes his dangerous encounter with a… | By Intrepid Sea, Air & Space Museum | Facebook

Raunchy Redskins…Ken Burns

Rescue Synopsis…HS-6 Raunchy Redskins Website

CHAPTER 7

SHINING BRASS

On October 12th, Lt. Deane Woods, call sign Canasta 572, was flying along route 15 near Lang Long when he was hit by AAA fire and suffered a fire in his starboard wing. Having nursed his aircraft until the fire became critical, he was forced to eject twenty-five miles inland. Immediately, the crew of Lt. Bob Burnand, Lt.(jg) Doug Heggie, AXC Kenneth White, and AX3 Roger Sitko were vectored to the area, and were able to establish radio communication with Wood. However, the crew did not have visual contact with the downed pilot. While trying to establish a visual sighting, Burnand and Heggie noticed that the main gear box temperature was exceeding normal parameters, but they ignored it, choosing to continue the search.

Still maintaining radio contact, Burnand was hovering over a heavy forested and brush covered terrain when the helo came under heavy enemy fire and soon found itself riddled by small arms fire. Quickly, Chief White and Sitko manned the guns at the port and cabin door respectively and provided retaliation to prevent the loss of their aircraft. Chief White was wounded in the exchange, but still urged Burnand to keep searching for Woods as a pencil flare smoke trail had been seen prior to the firefight with the NVA.

Despite the troublesome gear box and a wounded crew member, the search continued until the diminishing light of the impending night, low fuel, and increasing enemy activity forced them to retire from the area.

The following day, Burnand would lead a new effort to find Woods. Flying with him on this mission were Lt. (jg) Ross Mordhorst, AX3 Roy Powell, and AMH 2 Royse Roberts. Also, joining the efforts were Lcdr David Murphy's crew (Ens. Ed Marsyla, AX3 Steve Caple, and ADJ1 Vic Vicari).

For two days, both crews searched without finding Woods or having radio contact. Along the way, the JPRC (Joint Personnel Recovery Command) decided to become involved in the effort. The JPRC was a unit formed just the previous month, under the SOG (Studies and Operations Group) command structure and was given the mission to coordinate the recovery of downed or imprisoned US forces.

A team of operatives from SOG (Studies and Observation Group) North were flown to the Intrepid. The team consisted of several American Special Forces members and a group of Nung tribesmen. The Nung was a Chinese ethnic group from North Vietnam that had received poor treatment from the Communist North and were highly motivated to enlist in the struggle against them. The Americans called them mercenaries, but they were mercenaries with a deep hatred for their enemies, the Democratic Peoples Republic, and their army.

The SOG had started the Shining Brass Operations in 1965, placing American forces and American led forces into Laos, Cambodia, and North Vietnam. Many of its missions were aimed at interdicting the Ho Chi Minh trail and its supply lines south, while others were there to place a clandestine presence in enemy areas. Besides the Nung, other mountain tribe members known as the Montagnards were the main personnel and were led by US Special Forces.

Lcdr. Murphy and Lt. Burnand were selected to pilot the two aircraft that would insert the team. Flying with Murphy were Ensign Ed Marsyla, a diminutive young pilot with a powerful athletic build, the youngest gunner was Steve Caple, and the elder statesman of the group was veteran Vic Vicari. Vicari was a veteran of three wars and unflappable in the face of adversity.

They inserted the twelve-man team a half mile away from Wood's last known location, and took off immediately, giving the team time to comb the area. The team was on the ground for four hours when they contacted a North Vietnamese patrol. After a quick firefight, the NVA patrol were eliminated. However, the team leader surmised they had been compromised and immediately radioed for extraction.

The two H-3's were sent back to the insertion point and made radio contact with the Shining Brass team leader. As soon as they concluded the extraction plans, the helos approached their landing zones (LZ). For a while, the ground cover made landing a bit difficult. But just when they started hoisting the team aboard, they came under intense fire.

Marsyla, in Murphy's bird, caught the familiar smell of JP5 jet fuel and without hesitation, applied full power to the T 58 turboshaft engines from the engine control. Simultaneously, his aircraft was taking multiple small arm hits, so much so, that the stretched aluminum sounded like a metal roof in a hailstorm. Murphy issued the command to break hover and nosed the helo forward into forward flight, just as Vicari and Caple began laying suppressing fire. The quick actions of both the helicopter commander and his co-pilot prevented the loss of their craft and crew, although the fuel starvation of one of the engines caused it to lose power an eventually quit completely. The young Ensigns decision to apply power and Lcdr Murphy's breaking hover and starting forward flight had saved the day, but only for the moment.

Burnand knew that he would need to extract the remaining nine team members. Already, Murphy had three Nungs aboard and was racing towards the coast as fast as his one engine bird could go.

Burnand operated the hoist from the cockpit as his gunners were actively engaged with the enemy infantry. Gradually, the team was hoisted to safety. Finally, the last of the team got on the sling, Burnand's cue to break cover as Royce and Powell fired hundreds of rounds of M 60 ammunition into the enemy positions. Burnand and Heggie were soon in forward flight, while their gunners stayed alert to any tracer fire from the foliage below. Burnand's leadership and his crews' performance had saved the lives of the SOG team.

As Murphy exited at 3,000 feet, Marsyla watched the countryside below and noticed a tranquil village with a small schoolhouse and its grounds. Just then, the helicopter was buffeted by a burst of 37mm flak. The veteran Vicari saw the dark smoke bursts closing in on the helo and commanded, "Descend, descend, descend!" Once again, the crew was saved by immediate decisive action as Murphy raced towards the deck, but it was not enough. As the flak closed in on their position, it exploded, sending a burst of shrapnel that wounded all aboard, including the Nung, though they sustained only minor injuries. Vicari went to aid Caple who had been knocked unconscious by the explosion and left bleeding. Fortunately, Caple regained consciousness, allowing Vicari to examine the damage on the craft.

The skin of the cabin was punctured so many times that some sections looked like the metal on a screen door. When he investigated the pylon section, he examined the tail rotor control cables, and noticed that one had been hit and its wrapped wires were beginning to fail, one by one. Vicari told the flight station their chances were excellent that they would soon lose tail rotor control. Vicari began to photograph the area with a polaroid camera. The surviving picture would record over 200 hits their bird had suffered. Indian Gal 69 was quite a bird, and still showed a will to live as its crew limped over the coast.

Suddenly, the alert Marsyla smelled jet fuel again. Scanning the gauges quickly, he noticed the fuel in the aft tank was being emptied at an exponential rate, one that was very much visible. The self-sealing tanks were self-sealing in name only at this stage. Self-sealing tanks were made of rubber, both untreated and treated. The untreated rubber would absorb the fuel, swell, and close the puncture. However, the 37mm burst had torn holes in them that were too large for the untreated rubber in the tank to swell and close. So, Murphy headed for the South SAR Station fifteen miles away.

The USS Halsey at South SAR was immediately alerted to Indian Gal 69's plight. Quickly, the Halsey went to flight quarters, and Murphy's IG 69 was soon in visual contact. The Halsey laid in a course that would put the wind at 30 degrees off its port bow, while the Indian Gal 69 prepared for its final approach, carrying wounded men who were bleeding from eyes, noses, and ears, a result of the concussion obtained from their brush with the flak burst.

Murph and Marsyla, stood by the controls as the Halsey drew closer and closer. Then Bang! The final strands of the tail rotor cable snapped, and the helo began to spin on its axis. In the blink of an eye, the tail rotor control became an item on the crew's Christmas wish list.

IG 69 corkscrewing into the water, Murphy expertly guides the stricken plane and its injured crew and passengers into Gulf waters. Photo taken from the Halsey courtesy Raunchy Redskins, Ken Burns

However, the Indian Gal 69 would not go quietly. Murphy's hundreds of hours' worth of flight experience kicked in as he tried to mitigate his proud warrior's entry into water. He reduced power to the collective, which lessened the centrifugal forces driving the corkscrewing motion. Once in the water, he fought to keep it upright. The H3 was very top heavy with the 2 GE T58 engines and main gearbox above the cabin. If the aircraft tipped and inverted, it would spell disaster for the five (Nungs, Caple, and Vicari) in the rear as they would be tossed about like rag dolls in a pit bulls' mouth.

Vicari and Caple unloaded and inflated the survival raft, then Marsyla boarded it with the Nung. The raft would end up being a temporary bastion as it had been punctured during the battle. Marsyla was seen handing paddles to the Nung, and yelling the command, "Paddle, damn you, paddle!" However, the Nung could only look back with terrified expressions. They did not speak English, and though fearless on land, were now in unfamiliar surroundings.

The Halsey had put their whale boat into the water the moment the Indian Gal 69 landed. Fortuitously, it got to the struggling crew, picked them up, and transferred the Nung to the whaler. The H-2 helo with the call sign Clementine was in the air and aided in plucking Murphy's crew from the Gulf waters. IG 69, its boat hull punctured many times was slowly filling up with water and sinking. It had done all anyone could ask and was soon plummeting to a watery grave.

Woods was taken prisoner two days prior to the Shining Brass mission. It had been a futile attempt, but it was one that highlighted the commitment that America had to its fallen. He would not be released until March of 1973 and would later be married to a young lady that had worn his POW bracelet. The Air Wing aboard the Coral Sea had experienced a rough first 30 days of their deployment having lost nine planes, three F-4 Phantoms, three A-4 Skyhawks, two A-1 Skyraiders, and one F-8 Crusader.

Although Woods was not rescued, the courage of both crews involved in his rescue attempt resulted in the preservation of the valuable special operations team that was led by Richard Meadows. Meadows was a sergeant at the time of this mission. However, he was later given a battlefield commission and led the raid on the Son Tay POW camp later in the war for which he would be promoted to the rank of major. Earlier in his career, he had been an exchange NCO with the British SAS, one of only two non-British servicemen to be awarded SAS wings.

Lcdr Murphy would be awarded the Navy Cross, and the rest of the crew Silver Stars. All four crew members had earned Purple Hearts.

Lt. Burnand would also receive the Navy Cross, Mordhorst and Powell would be awarded Silver Stars and Roberts, the Flying Cross.

Lcdr Murphy facing left with his Navy Cross and Purple Heart, Marsyla, a Lt. (jg) in this photo, and Vicari awaiting their awards, not pictured Steve Caple. USN Photo

Notes:
Lt. Deane Wood comments on his loss in the POW synopsis
Vietnam Air Losses Search Results Canasta 572 Deanne Wood
Galdorisi, G. & Phillips, T. (2008) *Leave No Man Behind,* Zenith Press
Raunchy Redskins Rescue Synopsis HS 6 website, Ken Burns

CHAPTER 8

DIVERSIONS

In early Fall of 1966, Operations was alerted that President Johnson may need to utilize the squadron aircraft during the upcoming Manila Summit Conference because the president's VH-3 aircraft was at first thought 6 inches too tall to airlift on the transport aircraft, and other aircraft would need to be provided for secret service support.

Prior to the President's, arrival, the selected helos would be brought to a higher maintenance standard, and extra engine power, which the commander in chief's presence would require. The presidential entourage would include his personal pilots and staff.

However, prior to the conference, it was determined that the president's helicopter could be transported, but the squadron would still need to provide support. Lcdr. Nichols would fly the secret service sharpshooter and provide any backup service an emergency would require and was told the President was Job 1. When he asked if that would extend to the first lady, the secret service reiterated that the president and only the president was priority 1. Probably, that aspect was left out of the wedding vows a few decades prior.

Ferdinand Marcos, the President of the Philippines would be the host of the event, while other attendees would include the Prime Minister Nguyen Cao Ky (South Vietnam), Prime Minister Harold Holt (Australia), President Park Chung Hee (Korea), Prime Minister Keith Holyoake (New Zealand), Lt. Gen. Nguyen Van Thieu (South Vietnam), and Prime Minister Thanom Kittikachorn (Thailand).

The squadron would send six helos to the conference, to be housed and supplied from NAS Sangley Point on the south side of Manila Bay. They maintained a flight line and service area, separate from other aviation contingents at the base. The aircraft were reconfigured to airline standards, with white insulation covering the interior. The pilots would fly in khakis with their fore and aft caps, while the crew would be in tropical whites, wear headsets, and would have the opportunity to store their flight helmets for the time being.

Aside from secret service duty, they also provided transport for the visiting dignitaries, Madam Cao Ky, and van Thieu among them. These were the days of sight-seeing and flying. The Presidential staff issued those in the detachment presidential Zippo lighters as a memento.

Trouble on the O Boat

On the 26th of October, the USS Oriskany, an Essex class carrier still serving as an attack carrier suffered a horrible fire incident.

It was a normal morning. The galley and wardroom had just completed breakfast and the aircraft handlers, plane captains, ordinance men, and fuel handlers were preparing the morning attack launch. Given the amount of red-shirted ordinance men, yellow-shirted plane handlers, brown-shirted plane captains, etc., the flight and hanger decks would have been a pallet of color.

The launch the previous night had been cancelled due to poor weather conditions. So, the A-1 and A-4 strike aircraft on that launch were repositioned to the hanger deck to make room for the morning strikes and to offload flares and ordinance that had been prepared for night operations.

On the forward hanger deck, ordinance men were offloading bombs, rockets, and MK 24 parachute flares. The 24-pound flares were 2 feet in length and burned at 2 million candlepower. Brightness was achieved by burning magnesium with a high temperature that reached 3000 degrees Fahrenheit, turning night into day for the reconnaissance cameras and attack crews.

Two young sailors were tasked with stowing the unused flares from the previous evening, when one of them accidently dropped and was ignited by the safety lanyard. Each flare had a selection switch that could be set to armed or safe mode, and the safe mode on this one had not been activated prior to the flare being dropped. One of the young sailors quickly and inexplicably threw the burning flare into the flare locker and battened down the locker door. But also stowed in the same locker were 2.75-inch air to ground rockets containing composition B explosives.

The 3,000-degree temperature in the locker soon ignited flares in the enclosed space. The pressure inside the locker continued to build, until the locker exploded, producing a fireball that engulfed the forward passageways and portions of Hanger Deck 1. Then the munitions in the locker also began to explode initiating a cascade of destruction.

The passageways nearby served Officers Country, the portion of the ship reserved for officers of the Oriskany and the Air Group. Officers were struck down as the super-heated air seared their lungs, while others were trapped inside their bunkrooms. This portion of the ship contained mostly pilots from the air group.

In the hanger deck, two UH-2 Kaman helicopters were caught in the initial blast, rupturing their fuel cells, and initiating more fires inside the great ship. The secondary explosions helped spread these fires throughout the hanger deck area, the resultant heat causing a liquid oxygen tank to explode.

Officers were being trapped in their rooms as the fire spread forward through Officers Country. Those that had a porthole, opened it to gain fresh air. Some wet their bedding and wrapped their bodies in it to cool off in the blistering heat. Many of those trapped were overcome by the smoke, adding to the growing list of casualties.

On board the Constellation, was the SAR Detachment from HS-6. A member of that detachment, AX-3 Terry Hall, was on the ready crew waiting in the ready room. He had been assigned the 24-hour assignment and looked forward to catching up on some reading. As it was a reserve SAR assignment, he was the only enlisted crewmen tasked with it. Prior to breaking out the book, he took the escalator to the flight deck to pre-flight the ready helo.

"When I arrived on the flight deck I proceeded to the area where the helo was positioned," he related some 56 years later.

"I noticed everyone on the deck had their attention occupied with something over my left shoulder. Both of my pilots ran up to me and one yelled, "C'mon Hall!"

"Where are we going?" he countered.

"Over there," came the reply and Hall looked in the direction occupying all the attention. "I could see a carrier, engulfed in smoke. She did not appear to be a place I really wanted to visit."

While Hall and the two pilots performed a preflight, the crew of the Constellation loaded the helo with OBA's (oxygen breathing apparatuses). Then Hall's crew quickly took off and closed in on the Oriskany. "I think their helmsman turned her abeam to the wind to clear her deck of smoke for our landing," Hall explained. "She had smoke billowing from her."

When they landed, he noticed less panic than expected, though he thought there was a lot of confusion. He saw flight deck personnel scurrying about with a look of loss and saw men attempting to keep the danger to their ship at a minimum. "I noticed red shirted ordinance men deep sixing bombs and saw some aircraft smoldering on the smoke-filled deck. The crewmen of the Oriskany ran forwards and off loaded our cargo."

Then Hall went forward in the cabin until he was directly behind the pilots. He could see a yellow shirt before them. "He seemed to be in a daze and going through the motions of muscle memory. When he gave the fold rotor blade sign, I leaned forward and said to our HAC (helicopter aircraft commander) that I thought folding rotors was not a good idea in case we needed to leave the burning ship in a hurry." The HAC nodded and gave a cut sign with his open thumb across his throat, returning rotor blades to the flight position.

"By this time, we seemed to be a forgotten item, although we continued to maintain our aircraft ready for immediate flight. I watched the fire crews and rescue crews perform their duties. I watched as stretcher bearers moved inanimate bodies from one area on the deck to another. These men on the stretchers did not appear conscious, no movement."

Indian Gal 54 just landed on the Oriskany, crew hurries to offload OBA's. AX-3 Hall in Cargo Door behind gun mount. US Navy photo. USS Oriskany archives

"We were informed by radio that we would transport the CAG (Carrier Air Group Commander) to the Constellation. They brought him to us on a stretcher, he was devoid of movement, and I thought at the time he had obviously been killed. I believe we gave him transport in deference to his rank."

The Commander that HS 6 transported was Cdr. Rodney Carter, Air Group Commander of Air Wing 16. He was killed along with 42 others that day. A 44th victim would expire a few days later. Thirty seven of the 44 were officers, with twenty-five of those from the Air Wing staff, including Levy and

Ballesteri, who had been rescued by HS 6 earlier. A memorial service was conducted two days after the fire. Lcdr. Ford, from Attack Squadron 25, was buried at sea as per his wishes.

Hall continued, "When I was closing the cargo door a young 3rd class petty officer ran from the island and thrust a note into my hand. He had given me his parents' home address with a plea that I write to them and let them know he was fine, unhurt, and very much alive." This was the time before cell phones and instant messages. Obviously, the young sailor was worried that the damages would prevent the carrier's onboard delivery aircraft from transporting mail. "I wrote the letter that night, and weeks later I received a reply from his mother that they had heard from him by the time the letter had arrived. Later that year I received a Christmas Card from the family at my home in Iowa."

Hall and his crew had just witnessed the greatest threat to a modern aircraft carrier--shipboard fire. The fire on the Oriskany would be a precursor to a larger and deadlier fire aboard the super-carrier USS Forrestal. That fire would claim 134 lives with another 161 injured. Of the 71 aircraft in the air group, 21 were destroyed and 40 damaged. In less than a year, fire outbreaks would cripple two of the navy's proud capitol ships and seriously impact two Air Groups.

For HS 6, the mission continued. October had been busy. They had Shining Brass Missions, normal SAR duty, support at the Seven Day Summit, culminating with a trip to Malaysia on the Kearsarge to provide Presidential support when President Johnson visited Malaysia.

Those squadron members not on SAR Duty in the Gulf accompanied the Kearsarge, and in crossing the equator, invoked the ancient traditions of initiating those sailors making their first crossing. By doing so, they would forever be known as "shellbacks."

Notes:

The USS Oriskany (CVA 34) fire and munitions explosions sourced from Wikpedia.

Moser, D., November 1966, Life Magazine, *A Carriers Agony*

Gilbert K., February 1967, All Hands Magazine *Fire in Hanger Bay 1*

Email conversations with Terry Hall

Seven Days Conference, Raunchy Redskins site, Ken Burns

Stars and Stripes, *Manila Rolls Out Red Carpet for six World Leaders*, October 24, 1966

CHAPTER 9

THE END IS IN SIGHT

During October, the SAR duties of the squadron continued. The efforts to rescue Deanne Woods, which culminated with the Shining Brass Missions of Burnand's and Murphy's crews were still fresh in the minds when new challenges arose.

It so happened that during the Wood rescue effort, Major R.P. Taylor of the USAF 354th TFS, flying from Takhli Royal Thai Air Force Base, had been shot down 100 km (60 miles) northwest of the coastal city of Vinh.

That day was one of the most active and intense days early in the war as four search and rescue efforts were launched.

Though Taylor was lost in the Air Force zone of rescue, the SAR crews were spread too thin with similar efforts ongoing in other areas. However, Vann Goodloe's crew consisting of LT (jg) Buck Carlton, AX3 Ted Williams, and ADJ2 George Armstrong had intercepted Taylor's Mayday call and proceeded to his position.

Goodloe was vectored to a point 60 miles inland drawing enemy groundfire along the way. An Air Force Jolly Green HH 3E, flying from one of the bases in Thailand was also enroute. Upon reaching the scene, Goodloe contacted the Air Force rescue coordinator, and placed his crew in reserve, standing by to render any assistance needed. The Jolly Green successfully hoisted Taylor aboard their craft, and Goodloe and crew exited the area, drawing enemy fire again until they were feet wet.

Their effort was the farthest inland transit by a Naval helicopter to that date. The coastal areas the Navy had to cross were defended much more densely. Much of the enemy population, port entry areas, and industrial capacity were concentrated on the coast and the capital of Hanoi, and therefore received large assets of the North Vietnamese anti-aircraft capacity.

Goodloe would be awarded the Distinguished Flying Cross, while Carlton, Williams, and Armstrong would be awarded the Air Medal for valor.

L-R Goodloe, Armstrong, Williams, Carlton. Photo courtesy of HS-6 reunion archives Ken Burns.

* * *

On the 24th of October, the crew of Lcdr George Tarrico, Lt. (jg) Rick Grant, ATR2 Arnie Hardin, and AX3 Gary Smith were alerted to a Mayday call going feet wet. They immediately proceeded to the vectored location in time to see the stricken pilot descending in his parachute. The pickup was uneventful and soon the crew proceeded to return the freshly rescued aviator to safety.

Two hours later, that same day, the same crew was alerted to a Mayday. This call poised more risk as the downed pilot descended near Ile de Bac Ca, a known defended island. The crew took evasive maneuvers as they approached. Using the outlying islands to mask their presence, they quickly took the pilot aboard and egressed the area. The professionalism of their approach and their willingness to heed the intelligence that had been gathered on the area, allowed them to get in and out with minimum risk to themselves and the mission.

With this crew bagging two rescues in as many hours, the squadron closed out a very eventful October. With rotation back to the States nearing, the squadron continued through the final month, carrying out its SAR and logistics missions.

* * *

On the first day of November, Lt. Allen Carpenter of Attack Squadron 72 was tasked with an Iron Hand mission. The Air Force and Navy had been flying Iron Hand missions since the previous year to deter the mounting anti-aircraft capabilities of the North Vietnamese Army. Iron Hand missions were flown with an anti-radiation missile called the AGM-45 Shrike. The Shrike would home in on the radar beam emitted by the enemy and follow it to its source, destroying the radar, while aircraft escorting the

Shrike carrier followed up with strafing and bombing attacks. Air Force missions would be using the F100 or F105 airframes. Overall, these Wild Weasel airframes experienced a forty percent loss rate during the war.

An indication of the dangerous nature of these could be demonstrated by the Air Forces 354th Tactical Fighter Squadron, charged with enticing enemy anti-aircraft batteries, including guns and SAM, engaging the squadrons aircraft to expose their positions, and allowing other aircraft to attack the batteries and radar systems. They attempted to discover hidden batteries and attack them, much in the manner of a ferret attacking a nest. While it was a splendid idea, the danger in it was shown in a 45-day period in which the 354th would lose all but one of their squadron's aircraft.

On this day, Carpenter led an attack of three aircraft on the radar assets at Haiphong Harbor to aid in a photo reconnaissance mission. He successfully launched his missile but was hit by cannon fire while over the target. Immediately, he turned towards the Gulf and the magical safety of the feet wet call, but he began to lose control rapidly as the aircraft was being engulfed by fire. With all other options expired, he pulled his face curtain, jettisoning the canopy as the rocket motors in the Martin Baker ejection seat propelled him into the wind stream.

However, the area he was descending into was being used by numerous sampans and fishing vessels. His wingman from the Franklin Roosevelt (CVA 42) and a flight from the Constellation made a concerted effort to keep the fishing fleet at bay until rescue helicopters could arrive.

Lcdr. Gerald (Gerry) Griffin, his co-pilot, Lt. (jg)Bill Hobdy, and crew arrived just in time to see Carpenter being pulled aboard one of the fishing boats. The boat beached itself and its prize catch, ignoring the jets overhead and the helo approaching. Any fire now directed at the boat crew would endanger Carpenter. So, the rescue attempt reluctantly came to an end. The North Vietnamese had offered a reward of gold for the capture of downed airmen, and the boat crew were not about to let that pass. That promised reward would offset all their perils.

Carpenter would be imprisoned for the next 7 years and would be released in Operation Homecoming in March of 1973. During his time as prison in the North Vietnamese war camp, he was promoted to Lt. Commander.

Griffin and his unflappable crew were forced to face the heartache of seeing a fellow American taken and not returned to his family. It was an all too familiar feeling as the Soviets and Chinese continued to upgrade the enemy's anti-aircraft assets. Soon, they would have the Fansong Charlie (NATO Code Name) upgrade, bringing a much lower discrimination altitude to their system, which made it much more deadly.

On November 23, 1966, HS-6 were relieved by the 8 Ballers of HS-8 and began its voyage to California, making a stop at Yokosuka Naval Base in time to do Christmas shopping at the local base exchange.

For its efforts, the squadron was awarded the Navy Unit Commendation.

For exceptional Meritorious Service from 1 July through 23 November 1966 while embarked on the USS Kearsarge CVS-33, in support of combat operations against North Vietnamese forces. During this period, units of Helicopter Anti-Submarine Squadron SIX were continuously on duty, providing search and rescue services throughout enemy land and sea areas, in conjunction with combat strikes. Among the well defended areas in which multiple sorties were conducted to rescue downed airmen were the heart of the harbor at Haiphong, the densely gunned Fai Tsi Long Islands, and the heavily anti-aircraft concentrated delta areas of North Vietnam. Every rescue opportunity and rescue reconnaissance were prosecuted fully, without reservation, until successful, or ordered ceased by higher authority. Concurrent with their intrepid search and rescue operations, the squadron aircraft provided utility services to vessels in the strike force, plying daily and continuously the airspace of the combat area. During the period 23–27 October 1966, the squadron provided helicopter services in support of the President of the United States during the SEVEN NA-

TIONS CONFERENCE at Manila, Republic of the Philippines. Due to the extraordinary effort and competence of the maintenance personnel, the heavy flight load imposed by these multiple tasks in no way detracted from the continuous and effective pursuit of rescue duties. The officers and men of Helicopter Anti-Submarine Squadron SIX have made a major contribution to United States objectives in Southeast Asia. Their courage skill, and inspiring devotion to duty reflect great credit upon themselves and the United States Naval Service.

Signed Paul Nitze

Notes:
Phone conversations with Captain Rick Grant
POWNET.ORG Carpenter, Allen Russell
HS 6 archives Raunchy Redskins Ken Burns
Galdorisi, G. & Phillips, T. (2008) *Leave No Man Behind,* Zenith Press

CHAPTER 10

PREPARE FOR THE NEXT WESTPAC

Offloading after a successful Westpac (Western Pacific Deployment) is somewhat anticlimactic, especially when it occurs during the holiday season. Leaves were granted, wives kissed, children hugged, and the season of Christmas was magnified.

January came with a return to routine. It was time to say goodbye to many old friends, greet new transfers, and get back to duty. Training flights were scheduled, co-pilots advanced to HAC, 2nd crewmen stepped up to 1st crew positions, and so on.

Those entering flight positions were given one week of SERE (Survival Escape, Resistance, and Evasion) training, held at the North Island and Warner Springs, California facilities. The first few days were spent in the classroom, with the trainees eating whatever food they could find. The shellfish (barnacles) from San Diego Bay tasted as though they had not so gently been basted in fuel oil. The wonderful week culminated in the evasion phase where the class was challenged to successfully evade the aggressor soldiers and enter Freedom Village. Those doing so would be treated to a BLT sandwich, which was quite the prize after a week of very, very, scant food. For the following two days, the prison camp phase ensued, consisting of light beatings, isolation, interrogations from the "aggressor" guards, and generally a study-in-misery. A successful escape attempt would be awarded with a sandwich, although very few of these were given in the years the camp was in operation.

The Commandant of the camp was prone to give lectures on everything from imperialists policies to the beauty of a flower, interspersed with beatings. Those not making eye contact with the commandant were rewarded with hard open-handed slaps from the guards.

One of the most difficult phases for many in the prison phase involved being enclosed in an extremely small container, where most of the muscle groups in the legs and back would either go numb or send painful messages to the poor victim. The prisoner/student most susceptible to the box were those with a deep-seated claustrophobic nature, which was probably unknown to them prior to this event.

Although most passed their SERE phase with only a week of hunger as a souvenir, the stakes were high. They were informed failure to pass could mean an end to flight orders in the combat area and a possible revocation of security clearances.

So, the crews were organized and underwent training. Time at the idyllic base south of San Diego passed quickly.

North of Ream Field was the Marine Base at Camp Pendleton. The 130,000-acre base provided a plethora of air to ground gunnery training venues. There were major shipping routes just offshore of Ream Field, which gave the airborne sonar crews opportunities to track the freighters entering and leaving San Diego.

In retrospect, most of the aircrews' training were aimed at the primary stated mission of detecting Soviet submarines with only a few hours spent in any CSAR situation.

The members of the squadron also tried to keep abreast of the events transpiring in the Gulf of Tonkin. It was becoming apparent that the North Vietnamese air defenses were improving as new equipment kept arriving from Warsaw Pact nations, the Soviet Union, and China. Coupled with that, their personnel were obviously improving, and they didn't rotate. If one was an NVA gunner on an AAA mount in 1966, they were probably a gunner in 1972, or dead. Their experience stayed in the game. They were brave, dedicated, and experienced.

The 8-Ballers of HS-8 were getting rescues, but the rescue lanes over the coast were becoming much tougher, and fewer "feet dry" rescues were available. One of their more memorable rescues was in March of 1967.

A Vigilante RA-5C from the USS Kitty Hawk squadron RVA(H)-13 was on a photo reconnaissance mission when it was hit by ground fire. The pilot, RVA(H)-13's skipper, Charles Putnam was at the controls, and he quickly understood the aircraft was out of control. So, he and the bomber/navigator,

Lt(jg) Francis Prendergast, ejected. They were under 400 feet when they left the aircraft, and their chutes only swung a few times prior to impact.

Prendergast landed just offshore in water that was only a few feet deep but was soon surrounded by local militiamen seeking the reward for capturing downed airmen. Prendergast, like most naval aircrews, carried a .38 pistol. It was a relic of WW2; at the time, the navy had thousands of these pistols made, and called them the "Liberty" pistol. Some twenty odd years later, they were still being used, although mainly as a signaling weapon. Coupled with tracer ammo, they would signal a downed pilot or crewman's location. Prendergast also carried a hideout gun, a .22 caliber pistol. A militiaman quickly relieved Prendergast of his Liberty Pistol, but while he and the militiamen were standing offshore, four A-1 attack aircraft rolled in, guns blazing. The militiamen on the beach and the villagers with them soon began to disburse. Caught in the surf with the man that took his pistol, and one other with a rifle, Prendergast could see an HS 8 aircraft heading his way, as the flight of four led by Cdr. George Carlton swept the crowd away with 20mm cannon fire.

Prendergast looked at his two captors, and saw fear, surprise, and panic in their eyes. These were not regular army, but part time defenders, militiamen. The man with the AK submerged himself to hide from the four-attacking aircraft, but the man with Prendergast's pistol, though scared, was not given to hysterics like his comrade.

With most of the enemy under fire, Prendergast reached for the .22 pistol he had hidden, and pulled it from one of the pockets on his flight suit. His guard seeing this, aimed the Liberty pistol at him and pulled the trigger. Click! The hammer fell on an empty chamber. He uttered an oath, an oath that if Prendergast could have understood probably would not be repeatable to his mom, and pulled the trigger again, only to discover, to his dismay, that Prendergast had left two chambers empty. It was Prendergast's turn, and he did not miss. He placed the small caliber pistol in his adversary's face and pulled the trigger. The round entered the unlucky militiaman's face just above the bridge of his nose, and he fell like a weighted brick. Quickly, Prendergast grabbed his .38 and rolled to his feet. The militiaman's companion was emerging from below the water when Prendergast struck him hard in the skull with his .38. Senseless, he staggered, allowing Prendergast to grab his AK and toss it aside. Though the man was able to regain his composure and his weapon, he was quickly forced underwater by Carleton's Skyraiders before he could use it.

Carleton and his flight tried not to harm the crowd on the beach, not just for humanitarian reasons, but also to protect their own. If the rescue went south, they did not want the prisoner to be greeted by villagers enraged by the loss of people who they had known all their life. Carleton was experienced and his flight from VA-215 did journeyman work that day.

Prendergast headed away from the beach with his pursuer doggedly on his trail. The militiaman would bring his weapon to bear only to be driven underwater by Carleton's flight as the water between him and his prize was being churned by 20mm fire. The militiaman, not knowing that the fire was not being directed at him, was forced underwater again and again but bravely kept the pursuit to capture or kill, if necessary, the lone American.

Prendergast emerged on a sandbar and awaited the helo. The Big Mother from HS-8, seeing a change in their situation, swept in for the rescue, its crewman having taken out the brave and determined militiaman with its M-60 after he engaged the helo with his AK-47 and became a threat to the mission. They were now drawing fire from the foliage just beyond the beach. The pilot skillfully positioned his helo with the gun positions facing the beach, took Prendergast aboard, and beat a hasty retreat as the fire intensified.

Most aircrews that flew had a plan in place if they were shot down as well as how far they would carry that plan depending on the situation. Prendergast's situational awareness acknowledging the fear and panic in the man holding the pistol worked to his favor. It was a long shot, but it delivered. For his actions that day he was awarded the Navy Cross.

For extraordinary heroism on 9 March 1967, as a naval flight officer serving with Reconnaissance Attack Squadron THIRTEEN, on a combat mission over North Vietnam. After being shot down, pursued, and captured by a group of enemy militiamen and soldiers in the shallow, coastal waters off North Vietnam, Lieutenant (jg) Prendergast calmly and accurately assessed his dire situation and cunningly conserved his strength for a bold and extraordinarily heroic escape. Demonstrating the courage and alertness of a disciplined and well-trained fighting man, he seized upon a most dramatic escape opportunity which presented itself for, at the most, a few fleeting seconds. By his exceptionally prompt, daring, and heroic action at this moment, he succeeded in eluding his captors and was, shortly thereafter, picked up by a rescue helicopter. Lieutenant (jg) Prendergast's keen foresight, sound judgment and courageous conduct in the face of an armed enemy, were in keeping with the highest traditions of the United States Naval Service.

However, Prendergast's pilot, Cdr. Putnam, did not fare as well. He was last seen running on the beach with the North Vietnamese following behind. Later, the North Vietnamese stated that he was found dead on the beach. Whether he was killed during the capture or because of the deaths of the two militiamen that attempted to corral Prendergast can only be speculated.

The 8 Ballers had collected a few water rescues besides Prendergast before they were relieved by HS-2 and the USS Hornet. The procedure of an advanced SAR detachment continued as the Golden Falcons took over SAR duties and HS-8 and the Bennington were on their way home in April. The following month, the rest of HS-2 and their home carrier arrived on the scene.

On the last week of April, the SAR business started to get busy. The 24th, 25th, and 26th of the month would see twelve aircraft downed, four per day. Only four of these pilots were rescued, with the remaining being killed or captured.

The 26th saw the North SAR manned by Lt. Steve Milliken, co-pilot Lt (jg) Pettis, first crew AX2 Pete Sorokin, and second crew of AX3 Charles Sather. The crew were on site and circling near Haiphong when the alpha strikes went "feet dry." As soon as Milliken heard the Mayday cry, he proceeded to the vicinity of the strike aircraft.

The aircraft that was hit was an A-4 piloted by Lt. (jg) John Cain. After he was struck, he tried to get "feet wet" and headed towards the Gulf. However, his plane had other ideas and he was forced to eject near the Do Son Peninsula. The Do Son Peninsula was located just to the south of the main shipping channel entering Haiphong Harbor and was heavily defended. Immediately, the sky above the Do Son was dotted with Cain's squadron mates from The Golden Dragons of VA 192. These pilots had just suffered the loss of Lcdr Mike Estocin, who was lost in a SAM suppression mission. Estocin had been hit by a SAM and was last seen by his wingman, head down in the cockpit plummeting towards earth. He had launched his last Shrike ARM missile before the plane impacted. The North Vietnamese listed him as captured, but he was not released following the war. It is now believed he died in the crash. For his actions prior to that day, he would be awarded the Medal of Honor, posthumously.

The Golden Dragons were determined to prevent Cain from being a POW/MIA wristband. Also on hand were numerous F-8 Crusaders from Fighting 194, a companion squadron from the air wing on the USS Ticonderoga with Cain.

The F-8s would strafe the enemy positions one flight of four at a time until their ammunition was expended, whereas they would be relieved by another flight of four. The Crusaders were successful at reducing enemy fire by constantly pounding them with their 20mm autocannons.

While this transpired, two sections of A-1 Skyraiders were launched to function as RESCAP, while HS-2 launched a support H-3 to aid in the effort. With the A-1s on site and escorting the Big Mothers, the rescue process commenced.

Millikin used the seaward side of the peninsula to shield his helo, but when he turned, putting his crew between the island and the peninsula the enemy fire intensified. Large spouts of water erupted on the starboard side causing him to comment about the poor accuracy of the "Spads (A-1s)". Just then, he noticed his RESCAP had just begun their firing runs. Immediately, Sather, a Minnesota lad from Waseca, began to return fire from his port gun position. The instructions to fire in short bursts were lost to the moment as Sather held the trigger tight, burning through the first and second barrel, the only reprieve being the moment he stopped to change barrels. Now, he entertained himself with the thought of fishing for Walleyes and enjoying a Grain Belt beer if he ever got the chance.

Sorokin had lowered the hoist but was now concerned with a junk closing in from astern. Quickly, a Skyraider made a dry run towards the junk at 40 feet altitude, causing the junk's skipper to have second thoughts about collecting the reward offered for the airman. The co-pilot carried a Thompson, a

.45 caliber survivor from WW2. Pointing the business end at the enemy, he squeezed off a few rounds, calling out targets to the RESCAP simultaneously.

Sorokin, still on hoist duties, saw that Cain had positioned himself on the rescue seat and communicated that information to the front of the helo. As he raised the hoist, he noticed Cain was now clear of the surface, and attempted to communicate with the pilots so they could transition to flight mode. However, when he attempted to do that, he saw that his intercom cord had pulled free from the plug. Quickly, he tossed empty shell casings at Sather, getting his attention. Then, he waved his hand forward, indicating that they could now move. Sather relayed that to the Big Mother pilots immediately, and it broke hover and headed east. As the helo gained speed, Sorokin reeled Cain in as the helo gained speed. Soon, the air resistance began moving his prize behind the aircraft. Millikin looked at the airspeed indicator and saw that it was at 125 knots, the maximum recommended for an armored bird with the new upgraded gold striped engines.

The Crusaders and Skyraiders were still moving dirt on the island and peninsula with their bombs and rockets as Cain dangled behind the helo. The Skyraiders delivered four 750-pound bombs on the face of the hill. These bombs were in the earth-moving business as the impact caused the hillside to give way and slide into the sea. When hoisting the dangling Cain into the helo, Sorokin was taxed with pulling him in against the 125-knot air resistance. Finally, with muscles aching, he pulled Cain onboard. Cain, who had dangled in the wake of the GE T58 engine was slightly air fried but immensely relieved.

For the crew of the Big Mother, it was a job done well with the adversity with the intercom, 125-knot air resistance on his survivor, and handled his station in a manner that spoke of his professionalism. Sather stood at his gun and delivered belt after belt of linked 7.62 candy to the trick or treaters on his side.

Not all rescue attempts would have a happy ending.

Notes:

Michael J. Estocin. (2022, September 23). In *Wikipedia.* https://en.wikipedia.org/wiki/Michael_J._Estocin

Galdorisi, G. & Phillips, T. (2008) *Leave No Man Behind,* Zenith Press

Conversations with Charles Sather 1971

Veteran Tributes Francis Prendergast

Francis S. Prendergast: Pilot Was Awarded Navy Cross—Los Angeles Times (latimes.com)

CHAPTER 11

SAD DAYS IN CSAR

In January, while HS-6 was returning from leaves, transitioning into training mode, and we were still celebrating being in the USA, SAR duties in Vietnam continued.

On January 6, 1967, the USS Gridley had just arrived on the South SAR station after departing Subic Bay, Republic of the Philippines. She was a Leahy class Destroyer Leader, which displaced 7400 tons, with a helo deck that hosted one UH-2B "Hookie 2" aircraft. The aviation detachment came from Helicopter Combat Support Squadron 1 and was known as Detachment 3. The Detachment commander and Helicopter Aircraft Commander (HAC) was Lcdr Joe Brecka. His co-pilot was John McMinn. While the cabin held the two gunners, AMS 2 Robbie Robertson and William "Duke" Duggan. The crew was scheduled for a familiarization flight by morning, but events said otherwise.

A flight of F-8 Crusaders from the USS Ticonderoga was attacking a suspected ammo dump when one of their flight was downed. The flight leader called Mayday and the 1MC on the Gridley sprang the ship to action. "Sar Alert, Sar Alert, prepare to launch the Sar aircraft!" This was the crews first flight in the war zone, and they were going "feet dry."

Approaching the area of the downed pilot, Brecka could see flak bursts attempting to take out more of the flight, which now served as RESCAP. He had performed gunfire spotting duties with American destroyers and quickly compared the size of the burst with the 5-inch shells he had experience with. He immediately nosed over and headed for the deck. Brecka's airspeed indicator was pushing 150 knots when he went "feet dry'. At this time, the sun was sinking as twilight approached.

Suddenly, the little helo was immediately taken came under fire. Air bursts erupted around Brecka's bird, the pressure from the flak explosions buffeted the little craft, and shrapnel from the near misses penetrated the windscreen. Brecka was hit in the bicep and took one more to his flight helmet, cutting the restraining screw and dropping the sun visor over his eyes. Now, his vision impaired, but he was quite helpless to alter the sun visor as both hands were required to control the aircraft. So, he flew with his head tilted back to peer under the visor.

Shrapnel and small arms continued to pelt the craft, sounding like hail in a storm against its stretched aluminum skin. But Brecka did not need to hear the rounds; he could feel them as they impacted the rotor blades, sending shudders to the controls. McMinn's flight controls, on the other hand, were also rendered useless by small arms and shrapnel, impacting the collective at his side.

Meanwhile, the continuous fire severed some of the electrical wiring harnesses in the cockpit above the pilots. Caution lights signaling system failures were appearing everywhere on the panel. As if that was not enough, bullet rounds were hitting the bottom of the pilots' armored seats, and although they failed to penetrate the plate, their impact served as a notice to the pilots of their perilous situation. But the pilots were not the only ones in the aircraft taking fire.

Clementine, the H2 call sign, was in deep kimchee. Robertson was returning fire with his M60 mount, when it jammed, forcing him to mount the spare. As he looked aft in the cabin, he saw Duggan, who was firing an M 16 rifle, go down. He had been hit in the lower back, with the round going up, traversing through his chest before exiting.

Brecka knew they were in trouble. He had lost much of his instruments, the controls were vibrating violently, demonstrating damage to the blades, and he had a gunner down. From his headset, he heard the call from the jets overhead signaling that he was taking fire, and it was time to exit. He had been flying over a small road heading east, and upon the calls, did a hard turn and began his departure north. However, he began taking more hits. So, he rolled right again and headed towards the coast.

RESCAP advised him to get out of there and offered to escort him. Enemy fire began to subside as he flew east. But they had another problem on hand. The aircraft was becoming harder to control. It was obvious to him and McMinn that a blade was out of track. Flying in the wounded bird felt like a kid driving his dad's car over speed bumps placed closely together. In the cabin, Robertson was applying what first aid he could render to his wounded crewmen. He would place a battle dressing and apply pressure to halt the bleeding.

For a moment, Brecka contemplated landing in a rice paddy, but decided against it. He had a badly wounded man in the cabin, and his best medical care was not going to be in a prison camp or at the hands of an NVA medic. At the same time, Robertson was performing mouth to mouth on the deteriorating Duggan. He needed to get to medical care, and soon.

He briefly endured a brief spat of additional small arms fire, but soon cleared the coast and headed for the Gridley, which was steaming towards his position. The ship was preparing to take the injured craft aboard, as the helmsmen turned the bow into the wind to increase the amount of air moving over the blades when they approached hover.

It took both pilots to manhandle the bird to deck. When on deck, Brecka observed one blade horribly out of track, and as he killed the engine, ordered McMinn to apply the rotor break, bringing the rotor blades to a stop. It turned out to be an excellent call. When the blades stopped, the air flowing over the rotating wing ceased, therefore providing no lift. One blade was almost touching the Gridley's steel deck. If the pilots would have let it free spin while winding down, it would have impacted with the pylon connecting the main rotor area with the tail rotor, causing a possible catastrophic situation on deck.

The Gridley's medical detachment gently placed Duggan into a Stokes litter and carried him to the ship's sick bay. Awaiting them was the ship's medical officer, Dr. Lonergan, who began to work tirelessly to save the young red-haired crewmen whom friends referred to as Duke. Soon, the sailors serving on the Gridley received a call for a donor with Duggan's blood type. In a short period of time no less than 75 men had assembled themselves in the passageway, with rolled up sleeves, offering to help.

Meanwhile, sitting aft on the landing platform was Clementine, holed some 36 different times by small arms and shrapnel. The flak shrapnel had created multiple entries. Fifteen of those holes were in the blades, which had torn and ripped great chunks from the rotating wings. The fuel cells were leaking JP 5 jet fuel like a colander in grandma's sink. The self-sealing components were finally giving way to the reality of the situation. The avionics section was shot, control surfaces damaged, fuel cell heavily damaged. In short, it was unflyable and would be until it could receive a major rework at a proper facility. The Gridley would need to take it to a port as damaged cargo, crane it off the helo deck, before resuming duties in the Gulf.

After several hours, Duke Duggan's fight for life was over. He had only recovered consciousness once, to ask how Lcdr Brecka fared with his wound. Brecka was lucky; the shrapnel had torn flesh but had not penetrated the artery. Doc Lonergan had shared that the jagged shard had pushed on the artery without damaging it. He speculated that with all the exertions required to get Clementine back to relative safety, it was very fortunate the artery did not rupture. If that had occurred, Brecka may have bled out prior to landing.

The pilot that Det 3 had attempted to rescue was captured and interred until 1973. Mullins plane came apart shortly after being hit. Feet wet was never an option. Lt. Richard "Moon Mullins" would be a guest of the NVA, despite the great effort by Det 3 to prevent his capture.

Lessons were being learned on the fly. The infantry had learned you do not use paths or trails without expecting an ambush. The same lesson could be applied to helos. Roads make navigation easier; they also are a boon for the enemy to assemble AAA and troops. However, tougher lessons were ahead.

Notes:

Conversations with HC-7/HC-1 historian Ron Milum

Navy Helicopter Association, letters from Joseph Brecka to parents of William Duggan

Navy Helicopter Association, letters from Medical Officer to parents of William Duggan

Virtual Wall, comments from Lewis "Robbie" Robertson

Facebook HC-1 HC-7 comments John Birch

Galdorisi, G. & Phillips, T. (2008) *Leave No Man Behind,* Zenith Press

Deck Log of the USS Gridley furnished by Ron Milum

Damage chart of the UH-2 of Lcdr Joseph Brecka courtesy of Ron Milum

CHAPTER 12

SAR PEAKS AND VALLEYS

During the summer of 1967, HS-6 was enjoying the last few weeks before their deployment to Westpac, where they would replace the Golden Falcons of HS-2. Leaves were being taken, and final mechanical preparations were being performed to have all the squadrons aircraft ready to fly from Ream Field and join the Kearsarge.

Meanwhile, in Vietnam, the war continued. The bombers were tasked with interfering with supply to the south and the insurgents fighting the Republic of South Vietnam. The Ho Chi Minh trail, east of Vietnam and passing through Laos and Cambodia were the main targets of the Air Force, alongside the railroad marshalling yards, and POL (Petroleum, Oil, Lubricants) holding sites. They also conducted SAM and AAA suppression simultaneously. For the Navy, it was similar, although most of their targets were in the Western portion of North Vietnam, including the capitol of Hanoi.

In late May, a flight of Air Force F-4 Phantoms were conducting a strike on the railroad supply line from China, and the storage and yards near Kep. Two of the Phantoms were hit; one of them hit the ground immediately killing both crewmen aboard. The other, flown by pilot Major Richard Vogel and weapons officer, 1st Lt. Daniel Baldwin experienced heavy flak damage, and turned the nose of the stricken craft towards the coast, cognizant that the Navy performed nighttime SAR due to their antisubmarine training and doppler radar, while the Jolly Greens still lacked that capability in 1967. However, their aircraft had other ideas and the two crewmen were forced to eject north of Cam Pha, near the coast.

In the Gulf, the Bonhomme Richard (Bonnie Dick), an Essex class attack carrier, alerted their air wing for a nighttime SAR mission. The Air Wing would provide four A-1 Skyraiders for RESCORT and RESCAP duties, four F-8 Crusaders for MIGCAP, an E-1 (aka a Willy Fudd or Stoof with a Roof) for command and control, and one A-3 "whale" for inflight refueling capability. The A-3 was developed as a nuclear capable bomber in the 50s and due to its size and carrying capacity was now used for inflight refueling.

The helicopter asset would come from HS-2 SAR Detachment. Big Mother had flown on the North SAR most of the day and had just returned to the carrier when they were refueled and launched at 2100 hours for the 2-hour transit north. Upon reaching the area, the HAC, Lt(jg) Stephen Porch looked for a destroyer for HIFR (high inflight refueling) to top off his depleted tanks, but the rescue hoist gained a gremlin on the cable and was not 100%. Porch lowered collective and closed the altitude to the deck of the tin can, while first crewmen AX 2 Paul DeGennaro and gunner AX 2 Duane Shaffer lowered a line and hoisted the heavy fuel hose hand over hand. When it reached the cabin, one would brace themselves against the starboard gun mount while the other connected the fitting and opened the valve. It was not an ideal moment, but the mission was still on thanks to the cabin crew. Once fueling was complete, Porch contacted the on-scene commander, skipper of the A-1 squadron, Cdr. Carleton, who was no stranger to providing CAP to the Golden Falcons. Carleton had been in voice contact with Baldwin and ordered two of his Skyraiders to escort Porch. As they approached the mainland, they passed over several large, well defended islands.

The NVA, alerted by a plethora of radar signatures, began heaving softball size tracers towards the inbound trio. The helo and its escorts began to change direction and altitude frequently to prevent the enemy gunners from gaining a firing solution. Regardless, the fireballs continued to come in four or five round waves, lighting up the dark night.

Porch, zeroed in on an ADF cut he obtained from a survival radio and headed towards it. One of the Skyraiders warned him to veer off, explaining that he was heading into a trap. A North Vietnamese officer with an excellent command of English was using the guard frequency of 243 MHz to lure Big Mother into a killing zone. So, Porch veered off, avoiding disaster.

Some nights are darker than others and this night was of the darkest kind. The enemy gunners were using the rotor and jet engine noise to fire at the approaching helo. Helicopters were never called quiet, but this night the rotor blades must have sounded like a rock band to a big band aficionado. DeGennaro and Shafer stood at their guns. They had 2,000 rounds standing by for each gun, round in chamber, and were ready to provide suppression fire, but Porch ordered them to stand down for the time being. The string of 7.62mm erupting at 12 rounds a second with every fifth round a tracer would give the enemy gunners their exact position. Let them fire at noise, not sight. As the helo entered the area, DeGennaro was on the cabin floor, and leaned out to observe the tail rotor and advise the flight deck on any obstructions they may encounter nearby. Meanwhile, Shaffer kept an eye on the left side from his position. While the dark helped keep them hidden from the NVA, it also provided new perils. The Big Mother was just as blind as the enemy.

Carleton, who was orbiting above, saw the fire aimed at the rescue crew increase. He knew he had to provide suppression fire before the enemy hit the jackpot with a lucky shot, but he was presented with an enigma. Looking down, he could see the tracers on the scene, but couldn't see the helo. If his four Skyraiders began strafing the area, the chances of providing unfriendly fire to Porch and his crew were high, and it haunted his thoughts. So, he told Porch to illuminate his anti-collision lights for his flight to avoid perforating Big Mother with 20mm cannon fire.

Williams complied, turning on the red rotating beacon. The enemy replied instantly. Finally, they had a definitive target and began to riddle the helo with small arms fire. Carleton and his flight then rolled in, guns blazing, focusing on the bursts closest to the helo. However, Carleton quickly saw the intensity of fire that the helo crew was now subjected and gave the abort order.

Meanwhile, Porch continued to hold hover. His two gunners had both been hit in short order, DeGennaro in the arm and Shaffer in the calf muscle. Luckily, both rounds had passed through without striking bone, causing pain and bleeding, but manageable in the short term. Simultaneously, Big Mother was becoming a flying wreck. Rounds were coming through the floor, radio contact was lost, the helo began to yaw suddenly, and was going out of control. Fearing more danger to his craft, Porch immediately pulled out of the hover, and Carleton called off the effort. Now Big Mother had to retrace its steps. But the same large caliber AAA greeted their exit in the same manner it welcomed their entrance into the North Vietnamese air space.

Big Mother headed towards the cruiser Long Beach. In a white-knuckle approach, the two pilots skillfully landed the wounded bird. Fuel was pouring from the tanks as the self-sealing integrity of the gel was overwhelmed.

All five blades were damaged, some to the point of impending failure. A large hole appeared on the left side of the cabin, victim of a CO_2 bottle explosion after being struck with small arms fire. This Big Mother would be down and out of the fight for some weeks to come. The maintenance crew would need to spend many sleep-deprived hours to make it flyable again.

While this was transpiring, Major Vogel was invited to be a "guest" of the Democratic People's Republic, while Lt Baldwin was still at large and doing his best to avoid being Vogel's roommate at the Hanoi Hilton.

The following day, the crew of HAC, Lt Rich Daniels, co-pilot Ens. Lee Billings and gunners, AMS1 Massengale and AX3 McCoy, returned to the area. After a search, they located Baldwin and under fire took him aboard their helo. They had extended their fuel reserves locating Baldwin and were forced to kill one engine to conserve the dwindling reserve as they egressed the area. However, landing the craft with one engine was tricky. Given that it had restricted power, hover was out of the equation as it would require more power than was available with a single engine. However, Daniels stuck the landing better than a gold medal gymnast. When the remaining fuel was measured, he did it with three minutes to spare. Just another day at work.

When the crew of the Long Beach aided in refueling Daniel's aircraft, they boarded and flew it to the Kitty Hawk, the SAR Dets temporary home. It happened to be the only armored bird mechanically certified to fly so the very next morning it was back in the air, heading to North Sar Station near Haiphong. The Pilot was Tom Pettis, formerly the co-pilot on the Do Son rescue, co-pilot was Richard Hormuth, and gunners were PR2 Schmittou and ADJ 2 Ronald Soucy. As it happens sometimes in flight, a bird will take off and will not land. There was no radio communication indicating trouble, no debris found later, the Big Mother and its four-man crew were just gone.

* * *

On the 16th of July, the Phy Ly Rescue Saga would begin. Lcdr Demetrio "Butch" Verich was leading a flight of three F-8s in a flak suppression raid protecting a flight of A-4 Skyhawks hitting the railroad yards at Phu

Ly. As Verich and his flight approached the area, they were soon painted by Fan Song fire control radar, and surface to air missiles were on their way.

Verich immediately went into a split S maneuver, eluding two of the SA-2 missiles. However, the third and its 440-pound warhead exploded as Verich climbed 5,000 feet. The force of the explosion coupled with the speed of the fighter gave the pilot no options as his plane began to come apart in the air. Verich, who had been shot down almost a year earlier, ejected, and watched his Crusader disintegrate and fall to earth below him.

On the morning of the 17th, Lt. Neil Sparks, and crew were detailed to make the attempt to rescue Verich. Surprisingly, the first part of their flight was uneventful if crossing into enemy air space in a slow-moving helo could be referred to as uneventful. They approached Verich's position without significant ground fire. The area Verich was hiding in consisted of low farmland, rice paddies, and a plethora of villages, all in all, a populated area and population produced heavier militia strength.

The moment they entered a hover, what started out as peaceful quickly became chaotic as the area erupted with small arms fire, all directed at Big Mother. Gunners Al Masengale and Teddy Ray returned fire with their M60 mounts as their bird was hit again and again. In the ensuing exchange, they lost a generator which led to the loss of some of the avionics; the instrument panel was hit, along with the hydraulics closet just behind the flight station on the right side of the aircraft. Big Mother lost automatic stabilization making the helo difficult, but possible to control. Hydraulic losses were always serious. The H-3 had three hydraulic systems, primary, auxiliary, and utility. Loss of one was bothersome, but the backup systems would take over. Losing two made the pucker factor increase geometrically. Lose all three and the helo had the same flight characteristics as a refrigerator, except the crashing sound was louder and your next of kin would be notified by the chaplain.

Caught in the relentless barrage of fire, Big Mother took a hit in the avionics section in the lower nose. The Ultrahigh Frequency radio was gone. Using his survival radio, the co-pilot broadcasted on the guard frequency to both RESCAP and Verich. With comms now restored, they found Verich and soon had him in the cabin. Then they immediately vacated the area.

For his actions that day, Neil Sparks was awarded the Navy Cross. He had led his crew over a densely packed area of the Red River for two hours plus, plucked Verich from certain death or capture, and returned a damaged bird with superb airmanship and grit.

Notes:
Vietnam Air Losses Search Results LCDR Demetrio Verich
Thomas Edwin Pettis: Lieutenant Junior Grade from Alabama, Vietnam War Casualty (honorstates.org)
Galdorisi, G. & Phillips, T. (2008) *Leave No Man Behind,* Zenith Press

CHAPTER 13

THE SAGA AT PHU LY

The day after Verich was rescued, Lcdr Richard Hartman (USNA class of '57) flying from the USS Oriskany was leading a flight of A-4s attacking the railroad yards south of Hanoi when he got hit. He quickly nosed the Skyhawk towards the coast, but his plane was deteriorating quickly from the damage incurred during battle, and he soon had to eject near Phu Ly, a populated area near the Red River.

Luckily, he landed in a limestone hilly area to the northwest of the main population center. The limestone outcrops, known as karsts, contained a plethora of foliage, giving him better odds at evading capture than the rice paddies a few miles east of his position.

Overhead the sky was filled with fellow pilots from his squadron, VA 164. Many of the pilots were new, replacing losses from combat, normal rotation, and the Oriskany fire the previous October where four Ghostriders were lost. The little attack aircraft, affectionately known as "scooters" established contact with Hartman on the ground.

AAA fire, however, continued to be heavy and accurate. Soon, a second Ghostrider was struck by flak. Lt.(jg) Larrie Duthie, also attempted to gain the relative safer environments of the gulf but was forced to eject southeast of Phu Ly at Nam Dinh, another population area with many villages and hamlets in the countryside. The dwindling Ghostriders were also trying to provide support for Duthie when a third Ghostrider was struck.

It's pilot, Lt.(jg) Barry Wood was making a Zuni rocket attack when he noticed his fuel tank was going empty in a hurry. He immediately turned towards the gulf, nursing his wounded bird as far as its perforated fuel system would allow him. Then he called Mayday and ejected 'feet wet." The Richard Anderson (DD 786), a Gearing Class holdover from WW2, closed in on his position and executed the rescue.

While the Ghostriders battled for their messmates lives, the HS 2 Sar Detachment was scrambled from the USS Constellation. The HAC consisted of Lt. John Bender, co-pilot Lt. (jg) John Scholz, Gunners AX2 David Chatterton and AX3 Wayne Noah. Bender flew with an A-1 RESCORT from VA 152 and was experienced with many similar missions in the books. When the Skyraiders brought Big Mother to Duthie's position, they did not have a visual before hovering, so they could not be aware of the ambush. The NVA waited until their target was low and slow, then the foliage came alive with green tracers. With the enemy firing on all three sides, Bender found himself in a u-trap. A crew member sighted a smoke flare from the downed pilot, guiding Bender until he was over Duthie. However, swirling winds kept Chatterton from getting the hoist to the downed airman. With the enemy, closing in on Duthie's position, he had to take to the foliage. But Chatterton was persistent and kept trying to battle the swirling winds and the rotor wash before taking an enemy round to the chest. He went down, and it was obvious his wound was critical.

Bender's choices had just gone from slim to none. Duthie had been forced to evade the oncoming enemy and was no longer present, the hoist operator was down and needed immediate medical attention, and the airframe had taken multiple hits. All these forced Bender to break hover and abort the mission. The Locket flight from VA 152 was now augmented by a flight of Air Force Sandys, a group of A-1s designated for rescue duties. The Sandy commander ordered one of the Lockets to escort Bender out of the area, while he and his flight would work on the guns that had made Bender's life difficult.

The Sandys rolled in, one by one, delivering their bomb loads on the suspected positions. Soon, both Sandy 1 and his wingman were hit, but still operational. Sandy 1, Major Theodore Bronczyk, finished a run, only to find a MIG 17 in his wind screen, it's 30mm autocannons pounding away at the propeller driven Skyraider. The Sandys immediately dropped hanging ordinance and auxiliary fuel tanks to thwart the Mig jockey with sharp evasive maneuvers. Finally, the cavalry, in the form of Crusader MIGCAP arrived and the MIGS turned 180 and returned to their base.

The Migs had not gotten a kill on the Skyraiders but were effective in forcing them to dump ordinance and fuel. Sandy 1 and 2 were soon relieved by Sandy 3 and 4.

Sandy 3 had a Locket from VA 152 to escort a newly arrived Jolly Green HH-3E to the scene. The Lockets and Sandys on scene kept up the pressure on the NVA positions until their fire had diminished. The Jolly Green commander, Major Glenn York, rushed in, experiencing Zhu 23mm and 37mm AA fire on his crews' ingress into the area.

On the first pass, he overflew Duthie, but circled around and entered a hover allowing Sgt. Zerbe to lower the hoist over 250 feet to Duthie. Immediately, Duthie grabbed the jungle penetrator, unfolded the seat bars, climbed aboard and was on his way up. Major York, adding more power to the collective, brought the Jolly into a higher hover. Zerbe, in the cabin was still reeling in Duthie, when

York broke hover. As they departed, the Sandys and Locket aircraft were still ploughing the guns positions with Zuni rockets and 20mm.

Though Duthie was saved, AX 2 David Chatterton would succumb to his wounds on the flight out. Noah, his fellow crewmen, had performed the limited first aid that was available in the med box, but Chatterton's wounds were too severe, and Noah's best efforts could not change the writing in the sand.

The HH-3E had been constructed with one idea in mind, rescue. So, the hoist position was located just behind the pilot station, allowing better visibility for the pilots during the hoisting phase. The hoist had multi-speed capability. The HH 3E also had inflight refueling, demonstrated by a flight of two flying nonstop from New York to Paris. The landing gear sponsons to the rear of the hoist offered the gunners a slightly better field of fire than the Navy version. All in all, it was a much superior platform for rescue duties.

The crews were trained in rescue and proudly wore their ARRS patch proclaiming

"So Others May Live." And most importantly, they did not have another primary duty such as ASW. However, with all the difficulties presented, the antisubmarine squadrons soldiered on, risking life and limb to bring a fellow American home.

To add salt to injury, Richard Danner Hartman, the first Ghostrider to be downed was still at large. On the Constellation, Lt. Dennis Peterson, Ens. Donald Frye, and gunners AX2s Donald Magraine and William Jackson made plans for a rescue attempt. Fully aware of the difficulty the squadron aircraft had faced the past two days, they mapped out a route that would take them around known gun and SAM sites. The route as the crow flew would be a100-miles round trip, and they elected a 250-mile covert crossing. Once in the area, the darkness would shield them from the enemy, who they hoped would be fast asleep at the time.

Big Mother took off early, and began on the winding, circular route to the Phu Ly area, crossing the normally heavily defended coast without a peep or tracer from the darkness below. It remained quiet throughout the ride. When they approached the area where Hartman was known to be hiding, there was still no tracers from the blackness below. Frye was in radio contact and heard Hartman squawk, "You just flew over me." So, Frye told him they were coming around. Below, lurking in the dark, was a 37mm mount that took the approaching helo in its sights as it approached the hidden gun pit.

Then the night erupted in a crescendo of fire and noise. The first round struck Big Mother in the gut, igniting the fuel cell. Within seconds, the out-of-control bird crashed into a Karst outcropping, exploding on impact and four brave men were gone.

The powers to be, who had been observing the increasing air assets in the area over the past few days, became aware that five men had been lost. So, they made the hard decision; they had done all that was feasible, and Hartman was notified. The brave Academy graduate had successfully evaded the enemy for days. He, without sleep, food, etc. had been going on man's greatest motivator—hope.

Upon learning that he was about to be left behind, he broke and pleaded with his squadron mates still overhead, "Please don't leave me!"

Hartman was reportedly taken prisoner by the North Vietnamese authorities, and his remains returned in 1974. He had either been killed in prison camp or during the capture phase. The story his tormentors told was that he had been injured in the ejection and bailout. However, he was still well enough to actively evade an enemy bent on locating him.

For Peterson, one of the last photos of him showed a daughter, Kristin, being held by her dad in front of the Hornet. The following week after his death, he would be the father of another girl; this one named Denise, after Dennis, her dad. He would never get to give her away in marriage, watch them get dressed for their first dance, or hand them tissues when life threw them pebbles, but he gave them a legacy of courage.

Magraine's last photo showed him proudly holding his two young boys. There was a letter from his wife on the virtual wall, describing her difficulties in raising two young men to honorable manhood and how much his absence was missed.

Frye, the young man from Long Beach, was on his first assignment, and was proud of being a serving Naval Aviator.

Jackson was a Texas lad from Flores. His tanned good nature was a boon to those around him. His cruise photo showed the beaming smile of a brave man proud to serve.

The remains of all members of the crew of Big Mother 67 were eventually returned and interred together at Arlington National Cemetary.

* * *

HS 2 had a difficult cruise. The standard compliment consisted of 16 aircraft plus the 4 armored birds they inherited from the HS-8. However, they lost 8 of these aircraft to all causes, and thirteen of their squadron were killed.

A few days after the Phy Ly Saga, the SAR Det would transfer to the USS Forrestal.

The air groups of Task Force 77, and the flotilla of warships in the Gulf of Tonkin, were conducting a bombing campaign that had no parallel in American Naval History. Daily, tons of bombs were being dropped on North Vietnam to hinder their supply of weapons to the insurgents in the south, but the production of bombs could not keep up with demand. The navy's major ordinance used during this time was the 1,000-pound iron bomb. Their primary attack aircraft could carry two of these, or a single one-ton bomb. The number of targets hit could be doubled if the 1000 pounder was carried instead of the sole bomb. However, as the supply of newer bombs dwindled, the Navy reached deeply into its bunkers and began to use older and older ordinance.

On July 28th, the Forrestal received a shipment of "fat boy" bombs, some 13 years old. These used a composition B explosive that was inherently more unstable at heat than bombs they had been using. As if that was not enough, they also had to deal with Zuni rockets, which had a record of electrical malfunctions and could fire on their own.

Early July 29th, an alpha strike was being prepared on deck. On the stern of the Forrestal on the starboard side, several F-4 Phantoms were preparing to taxi and launch, while straight across from their location a group of A-4 attack planes were doing the same. Without warning, Phantom number 110, flown by Lcdr. Bangert and Lt. (jg) McCay, had a power surge, and mistakenly fired one of their Zuni air to ground rockets. The Zuni rocket contained a safety pin connected to a lanyard that would need to be pulled prior to launch. However, that pin had not been pulled, so it prevented the warhead from exploding. The rocket did puncture the fuel tank on the attack plane of Lcdr. Fred White though. The JP-5 jet fuel released from the punctured tank was ignited by the Zuni rocket motor and the fire spread. The rocket damage also spread to the A-4 just forward of White's aircraft and ignited the auxiliary fuel tank of A-4 no 416, flown by Lcdr John McCain.

One minute after the Zuni fired, fire quarters was ordered, and general quarters was sounded at 10:53. The fire quickly escalated as it was being fed by a 35-knot wind and the jet exhaust from planes preparing to launch. It spread along the deck as more fuel poured from the two Skyhawks. At 10:59 the bridge ordered, "Set condition Zebra!" –the order to close all hatches throughout the ship for maximum integrity.

Damage control team 8 was the first to respond. Chief Farrier led the team and began to put a smothering foam agent on the fire. A Korean era bomb fell from one of the stricken Skyhawks and began to baste in the growing fire. The damage control team had been instructed in the more modern bombs which did not contain Composition B and believed that they had a full ten-minute prior to explosion. Farrier continued fighting the fire with the PKP agent, allowing time for the pilots strapped in their planes to egress to safety. Suddenly, he noticed the bomb glow up in a bright flame, and understood it was cooking. He immediately ordered his team to withdraw, but it was too late. The 1000-pound bomb exploded, taking his life and all but three of his team. Another team was decimated at the same time. McCain was wounded in the bomb explosion while White was killed.

The bomb blew a hole in the flight deck and into the berthing compartments below. Burning fuel now poured through the hole and entered the ship. More and more of the bombs started cooking off. A total of ten would explode during the event.

Forrestal damage control party peers into the punctured flight deck in the aftermath of bomb explosion. USN photo

The deck was holed seven times by exploding ordinance and 40,000 gallons of jet fuel either went up in flames or poured into the interior of the ship via the bomb damage.

Sailors, most without damage control training, went to work, and began to roll ordinance off the flight deck and into the Gulf. They also pushed aircraft away from the growing conflagration. Two of the carriers' escorts, destroyers Rupertus and George McKenzie directed their fire hoses on the carrier while pulling sailors that were blown overboard to safety. The fire was finally brought under control as explosive ordinance teams began to deal with the damaged bombs and rockets left in the wake of the destruction.

The medical staff was overwhelmed, and arrangements were made to rendezvous with the hospital ship, USS Repose.

The fire killed 134 men, including two from HS-2, ADJ-3 Edward Dorsey, and AN Johnnie Frasier, while 161 more were wounded. The air group suffered heavily. Seven F-4's, eleven A-4's, and 3 RA-5 Vigilantes were destroyed. Forty other aircraft were damaged. Of the 73 total aircraft compliment only 12 was mission capable after the fire.

HS-2 had the bulk of the squadron on the Hornet, making a liberty and maintenance call. However, with its earlier losses, its mission load had naturally decreased. They were ready for relief and home. So, they awaited HS-6.

Notes:
Naval Aviation News, October 1967, *The Forrestal Fire*
USNA Memorial Hall Richard Hartman
https://va-164.org/events.htm
info on helicopter incident 151538 www.vhpa/kia/incident/670719.html
Defense POW/MIA Accounting Agency.
CDR Richard Danner Hartman
Galdorisi, G. & Phillips, T. (2008) *Leave No Man Behind,* Zenith Press

CHAPTER 14

HS-6 RETURNS

On the 18th of August, the USS Kearsarge embarked on its second war cruise of the Vietnam War. An advanced group, led by new executive officer, Cdr. F.X. McCarthy was sent ahead to the USS Hornet to relieve HS 2 of SAR Duties. On October 6th, the detachment formally assumed CSAR and transfers to the USS Intrepid. Soon after, like homeless orphans, they crossed deck again to the USS Coral Sea.

On log missions, training flights, or other times the flight allowed, crewmen threw out a flare and made M-60 firing runs to keep gunnery skills sharp. "First on the target gets to play again," said the instructor. An HS-6 crewman trying to make life difficult for a poor unsuspecting flare. Photo courtesy of HS-6 Raunchy Redskins site

On August 9th, an A-4 Skyhawk from the Oriskany and squadron VA-164 was hit while attacking a pontoon bridge at Nao Quan, North Vietnam. The pilot Lt.(jg) Laurence Cunningham immediately headed towards the coast. The smile on his face when he went "feet wet" soon disappeared when his engine flamed out. Cunningham started the restart procedures he had practiced multiple times in training, but it was an exercise in futility and he ejected as he dropped below 3,000 feet. Cunningham had stayed with the aircraft till he was outside the entrance area to Haiphong Harbor.

Lcdr George Cagle (HAC), Lt.(jg) Jerry Smith, with crew of ADJ-2 George Armstrong and AXAN Alan Nobles quickly swept in, dropped the hoist, and brought Cunningham back to the warm wishes of his squadron. The operation was unopposed. It was a nice beginning.

* * *

On the 23rd the detachment was cross decking to the Kearsarge when the aircraft Tom

Goen was crewing lost power immediately after taking off, plunging into the water below. The night was a particularly black one, and the aircraft was loaded with mechanics tools, spare parts, etc. along with a few passengers.

In the water, Goen became concerned that one of the younger sailors did not exit the aircraft, and briefly reentered to locate him. At that moment, the top-heavy craft inverted capturing the affable petty officer under the cargo that was in the cabin. His squadron searched feverishly, but to no avail. Tom was gone. The quiet hero, that only recently was awarded the Silver Star for actions in the previous deployment, left a wife and young daughter. He also left a squadron of friends. A memorial service was held aboard the Kearsarge.

* * *

On the 26th of October, Lt. Rick Grant, co-pilot Dave Weighton, with 1st crewman Petty Officer John "JR" Kitts scored a double—two separate rescues on a single mission, while under intensive enemy fire. The first was an Air Force jockey from the 354th Tactical Fighter Squadron flying from Thailand, who was hit while he was striking Kep Airfield east of Hanoi. Captain Martin Scott knew he was much closer to the Gulf than his base in Thailand and flew east until he was over water. But his Thud chose that moment to flame out from a loss of oil pressure. However, he was rescued without incident.

Crew of Linskey, Wahl, Weighton (top), and Grant

Later, Lt.(jg) Ralph Foulks from Attack Squadron 163 from the USS Oriskany was hit by AAA fire, but also managed to reach the Gulf and was rescued. However, his rescue was not a lasting fairytale. Less than two months later, Foulks was killed on January 5, 1968, when his Skyhawk (call sign Old Salt 303) was shot down on a nighttime reconnaissance mission over the north. His remains were returned in 1988. Those who did not know before, were becoming aware, the air war in the north was becoming a real meat grinder.

* * *

HC-7, a new face on the scene, relieved HC-1 of CSAR duties in the Gulf. The mega squadron of HC-1 had grown from its fleet angel duties to a goliath comprising 250 officers and 950 enlisted men. Their duties included Operation Game Warden duties flying UH-1 (Huey) gunship detachments in the Gulf in an exercise called Operation Game Warden. They were also tasked with Combat SAR duties on both the North and South SAR stations with Clementine UH-2b aircraft. As if that wasn't enough, the squadron had detachments of vertical replenishment aircraft (H-46) embarked on supply ships. Mission creep had existed prior to the war, but it was a bull rush event after the United States increased their involvement.

The Game Warden duties in the Mekong Delta was transferred to a new squadron,

Helicopter Light Attack 3, also known as the Seawolves. Then the Clementine duty went to the newly formed HC-7, also known as the Sea Devils with their main base in Atsugi Japan and a support base at Cubi Point in the Philippines.

* * *

On the 16th of December, Lcdr Steve Coakley, co-pilot Lt. (jg) Bill Medley, AX3 Russell Sprague, and AXAN Randall Amero were flying the normal racetrack pattern, also known as boring holes in the sky, when Sundown 101, an F-4 Phantom with the 'Freelancers" of Fighting Squadron 21 flying off the USS Ranger called Mayday. The Ranger had only returned to Task Force 77 for its 3rd war cruise on the 3rd of December.

The fighter crew, pilot Lcdr Diego "Duke" Hernandez and RIO Lt. (jg) Stephen Van Horn were performing flak suppression duties when they were hit. As the air battle raged on, the crew noticed their systems failing. Hernandez was then forced to control his crippled craft with rudder alone and nursed it seaward. Once they were feet wet, Hernandez made the decision to eject and alerted Mayday at 1300 hours.

Both the Big Mother crew and a Clementine crew from HC 7 (Lt. (jg) Timothy Melecoski, Lt. (jg) James Brennan, AMH-2 Gary Fleck, ADJ-3 Gary Schwake were vectored to the area. They arrived on the scene at 1310 and by 1315 both Phantom airmen were aboard the helos; Hernandez was picked up by Clementine and Van Horn by Big Mother.

However, Big Mother soon came under fire from shrapnel falling from an airburst that had been directed at Hernandez's F-4. They immediately took evasive action to avoid the crippled fighter. At 13:22, Coakley and his Big Mother crew land on the Coontz, and Van Horn was sent to the medical bay. At 13:25, three minutes later, the Clementine aircraft landed as the H-3 departed and Hernandez was taken to the medical officer for examination. There, it was determined he had suffered ejection injuries at the lower back and neck. Hernandez would be forced to eject again four months later, but again would be rescued.

The following day, on the 17th of December Lcdr George Cagle, Lt. (jg) Jim Payton, AXAN Alan Nobles, and ADJ-2 George Armstrong were launched due to an alert by an S2F (Stoof) aircraft from VS-29 that two downed Air Force crew were found close to the North Vietnamese shore. The Air Force crew, pilot Major Laird Gutterson and Weapons Operator, 1st Lt. S.P. Sox were from the 497th Tactical Fighter Squadron flying out of Udon, Thailand, and were shot down while attacking the Hau Hung Ferry.

Big Mother successfully located the downed airman and got them into the cabin while under machine gun fire from the coast. Cagle and Payton eluded the incoming rounds and exited the area.

Some rescues were memorable for those who were successfully saved. In this case, the pilot Gutterson had been in the Air Force since 1943 when he enlisted with the hope of learning to fly. He was sent to flight school as an enlisted candidate and would fly B-25s until the war ended. In the Korean war, he transitioned to F-51 Mustangs and the F-86 Sabre. Following the war, he became an Air University Lecturer, with a specialty in POW conduct and techniques that would be used in interrogation. He developed a manual on teaching the POW Code of Conduct.

Two months after HS 6 rescued him, his F-4 Phantom fell victim to an air-to-air missile launched by a MIG 21. He ejected near Haiphong, but rescue was not an option here. He and his weapons officer, Myron Donald, were taken prisoner.

Gutterson was kept in solitary confinement for over two years, and his training in interrogation tactics aided him in resisting the psychological and physical abuses the North Vietnamese meted out on him and other prisoners of war. One of the things he recounted that kept his spirits alive was the fact that he was sure his country would not forget him. His faith paid as he was released in March of 1973.

On December 27, 1967, the F-4B (Rock River 203) flown by pilot LT J.F. Dowd, and his radar intercept officer (RIO) LT (jg) G.K. Flint were making a weather reconnaissance flight near Haiphong when they were struck by anti-aircraft fire. The cockpit rapidly filled with smoke, and they turned the aircraft towards the friendly waters of the gulf, ejecting near the Fai Tsi Long group, and dropping into the cold water of the northern gulf.

Rock River 203 from Fighting Squadron 161 (Chargers) landing on the Coral Sea. Lt. Dowd and Lt. (jg) Flint's aircraft USN photo

A couple of A-1 aircraft from Attack Squadron 25 were soon overhead, providing cover. Lcdr Bolt and Ens. Ramsey began the search to get a visual sighting on the downed pilots, while Lcdr Rousa and Lt. (jg) Dunn rendezvoused with Big Mother 71, flown by

Lcdr Jim McGill and LT (jg) Gordy Thomas. AX2 Roger Sitko and AX3 Curtiss Williams had their M60s mounted. However, on this day, they would not be needed as their enemy was the cool water that the Phantom jockeys found themselves. After the rescue, they commented it went like clockwork, but with the cold water it was a terribly slow clock.

After the rescue, Big Mother 71 took the downed pilots to their home carrier, the Coral Sea. They arrived just in time for an alpha strike recovery under low visual conditions. Big Mother was directed to a spot on the deck where they offloaded their cold cargo. Thomas would later remark that they were cognizant of the recovery situation. No sooner had the helo pulled collective and rolled left than Thomas noticed an A-4 resting in the area they had just vacated.

The Coral Sea was also in the middle of hosting the Bob Hope Christmas Show for the troops. Thomas looked at the island and saw a Welcome Raquel sign. The Big Mother crew ended up missing the Raquel Welch sighting.

December also saw the Kearsarge, and the bulk of the squadron visit Sasebo, Japan. This visit would start off with a note of sadness as the great ship entered port under the klaxons of "General Quarters" as a fire broke out in the enlisted berthing area under hanger deck three. Given the disastrous fires that had happened in the previous months, this was a matter of concern. Damage control parties soon gained the upper hand, although not before three members of the ships company were killed and several more injured. On Christmas Eve two days later, a fire and explosion also struck the Adams class destroyer USS Lynde McCormick (DDG-8), injuring two sailors and demonstrating again that shipboard life on a warship was not for the fainthearted.

With HC 7 inheriting the CSAR duties from HC 1 and prepping up for the H-3 CSAR operations, HS-6 found themselves on the downhill side of the deployment.

Notes:
Galdorisi, G. & Phillips, T. (2008) *Leave No Man Behind,* Zenith Press
HS-6 Raunchy Redskins, Ken Burns webmaster
HS-6 Rescue synopsis. HS-6 Raunchy Redskins

CHAPTER 15

FINAL CSAR DAYS FOR THE INDIANS

The Sundowners from Fighter Squadron 111 boasts a long and distinguished history stemming from the late 1942 days when they were mustered into service, flying the venerable F4F Wildcat against the Japanese in Guadalcanal. The beginning of the new year in 1968 found them aboard the USS Oriskany, fresh from the yards after repairing the horrific fire damage by a flare. She had been on station since July.

The Air Wing of the Oriskany, Carrier Air Wing 16, lost 39 aircraft on this deployment. Twenty-nine to combat and another ten to operational losses. The high rate of loss has been attributed to several causes. For one, there was the heavy pace of their operations (9,500 sorties including over 180 strikes in the heavily defended Hanoi-Haiphong area). The second cause was the political decision to limit the bombing to certain areas. This action provided safe havens to the North Vietnamese and allowed them to intensify their defenses in the areas still open to attack.

On the 2nd of January, an F-8C from the Sundowners suffered an electrical failure while serving as MIGCAP on a photo-reconnaissance mission near Than Hoa. The pilot, Lt. (jg) Craig Taylor, nursed his aircraft to the Gulf of Tonkin but was forced to eject near the Vietnamese coast and amid a Vietnamese fishing fleet. His story would have probably met its end if Lcdr Leo Keiffer, co-pilot Lt Ed Marsyla, AX2 Thomas Munroe, and AXAN Danny Abbott had not swept in and snatched the prey away from the bounty-seeking fisherman. However, Craig would be killed in an operational accident at Naval Air Station Miramar on June 27 of the same year. He had been a USNA graduate from the class of 1965.

* * *

On the 10th of January, Lt. Bob Wildman, c/p Lt (jg) Don Sanborn, AX2 Jarvis, and AXAN Larry Wahl had a busy but productive day rescuing two pilots on separate occasions while on a logistics flight. While the destroyers received their mail and personnel, the crew returned two wet, but incredibly happy pilots to their squadrons.

The following day, the same crew except for Arnie Bruflat sitting in the co-pilot's seat, were alerted to the Mayday call coming from Lcdr D.R. Weichman.

Weichman, flying from the Oriskany with Attack Squadron 164, had been bombing the Ho Chi Minh Trail as a part of Operation Steel Tiger. The intense bombing campaign in Eastern Laos was an attempt to interdict supplies and personnel from being transported from North Vietnam to the South. As the ground war began to more and more to involve more troops from the People's Army of Vietnam (PAVN), it became more important to slow that flow. As early as 1965, it had been estimated that the PAVN was transporting between 4 and 5 thousand men along with 300 tons of supplies each month.

On this day, he was tasked with attacking a bridge near Ban Dong Pan in Southeastern Laos. He had already made two bombing runs and was completing his third when he felt his aircraft hit by small arms fire, and immediately decided to return to the Oriskany.

However, his engine began to vibrate, and he observed his temperature gauge going north. He still stuck with his hurt bird until it began to burn. Then he ejected over the Gulf.

Weichman was not a stranger to danger. He had begun his aviation career in 1955 as a Nav Cad cadet. He initially flew A-1s and later was a flight instructor. In 1964, he became an advisor to the South Vietnamese Air Force. While in that duty, he also flew C-123 cargo planes delivering supplies and saboteurs into North Vietnam. Then he returned to the Navy and transitioned into the A-4 Skyhawk. He had just been launched from the Oriskany when the disastrous fire broke out. Earlier in this cruise, his squadron mate Richard Hartman was lost.

Wildman and his crew vectored to Weichman's location. Still elated by the previous day and the chance to add a hat trick of rescues to the cruise, he and Bruflat concentrated on their course, nursing every bit of speed they could from their bird. Meanwhile, in the cabin, the crew went about installing and checking their gun mounts.

While waiting in the water, Weichman became aware of boats trying to close in on his position. Meanwhile, members of his squadron tried to protect him by repeatedly strafing the oncoming enemy. Weichman also became aware that he had a growing pain in his leg. Unknown to the 6'5 pilot, he had sustained an injury while ejecting. Later, it would be determined that he had broken his leg.

While he awaited rescue, he kept a wary eye on the boats that were still intent on his capture, and his fellow pilots just as determined to prevent that. Then his mind began thinking of what was in the sea with him. Every person that had flown had seen great schools of Hammerhead sharks throughout the Gulf, but what occupied and haunted his mind more this day was the seven varieties of venomous sea snakes every sailor had seen in the wake of the ship. During their mating season, thousands could be seen on the surface. When asked by his wife, later, if he was afraid of sharks, he would tell her he was much more concerned with the snakes. Right at that moment, time was going very slowly.

Meanwhile Wildman and crew, flying as fast as his tired bird could muster, entered the area, and visually located their man. Jarvis manned the hoist with Wahl assisting, and soon they had Weichman aboard. Then they broke hover and contacted the carrier that they were inbound and would need a medical team. Now, the crew could be happy and satisfied that they had bagged three pilots in the last two days.

Weichman being taken to sick bay as the roof rats of the Oriskany look on. Photo courtesy of the Raunchy Redskin site

* * *

On the 25th of January, HS-6 would conduct its final combat rescue. They were pre-stationed on the USS Dewey as a temporary replacement for HC-7, who had suffered a loss a few days earlier. The Clementine aircraft was on a training flight and the gunner, Petty Officer "Combat" Conlin was preparing for gunnery practice. However, when he closed the latch lever, a worn sear gave way, allowing the weapon to discharge into the H-2's rotor blade. The blade folded like a linen napkin and soon the Clementine crew was in the water. A motor whaler from the Dewey quickly rescued the crew, although that left the Dewey one helicopter short. Until a replacement could be sent from Cubi Point, HS-6 would need to fill in. On the 25th, that void was filled by the crew of Lt. Vernon von Sydow, Lt. (jg) Jim Rooney, AX-2 Johnny Jones, and AXAN Roland Cockerham.

For most of the day it was quiet, with the crew performing housekeeping duties in the cabin and the pilots monitoring radio traffic in Combat Information Center (CIC).

On the destroyer gunline, the HMAS Perth (D38), a former U.S. Adams and an American Gearing class U.S.S. Bordelyn (DD-881) were tasked with degrading highway communications south of the port city of Vinh. On the 25th, they were shelling a bridge when they came under fire from coastal batteries defending that area. The Perth and Bordelyn were sailing in formation, with a one- and one-half mile space between them. It was safe for a while, until the incoming rounds got intense as no less than thirty rounds began churning the waters near the ships.

Captain Peter Boyle, Royal Australian Navy, and ranking officer of the small flotilla, quickly put in a call for air support. The Aussies had been on the line and under fire before, as the pundits from the American West would say, "This wasn't his first rodeo." The cavalry dispatched was a flight of four A-4 Skyhawks from Attack Squadron 153, led by their commanding officer, Cdr. Thomas Woolcock. The flight from their carrier, the Coral Sea (CVA-43) was quick, and they were soon dropping ordinance on the NVA gun positions. Also in the area were North Vietnamese SAM batteries, armed with the SA-2 soviet missiles and Fansong fire control radar. Woolcock's aircraft was soon struck by a SAM, and he headed his crippled craft to sea., He had to eject just off the coast. When his parachute drifted to earth, he found himself ten miles from the destroyers and five miles from the unfriendly shore.

On the Dewey, the SAR crew were busy with the evening meal. The enlisted were standing in the chow line while the officers had just sat down in the wardroom. At 1818, the SAR alert was sounded, and the crew scampered to their aircraft perched on the helo deck. As the flight crew readied their aircraft (Big Mother 73) for flight, the Dewey helmsman put the ship in a hard turn to place the optimum amount of wind over the deck. The helo deck soon became awash with deck crewmen slipping and falling and the helo tugging hard against the tie down chains. Luckily, the chains had not been released or they would have been in danger of sliding into the Gulf of Tonkin.

While Big Mother was on the helo deck, the flight crew awaited the ASE equipment to heat up prior to take off. Jones and Cockerham in the cabin mounted the M-60s, prepared the first aid box for use, strapped the M-16s on the armored seats for immediate use by the pilots, and were soon airborne at 18:21 hours. Harbor Master II gave von Sydow a vector of 222 degrees and 37 miles to Woolcock.

Lt. (jg) Rooney initially had the aircraft and was soon closing in on the target at 120 mph, the maximum he could coax that required 90 % torque and tremendous vibrations. Lt. von Sydow was handling the communications with Harbor Master II and Powerhouse 305, Woolcock's wingman. Rooney maintained a height of 500 feet to facilitate better communications. As Big Mother approached Hon Mat Island, he descended to 100 feet to avoid the fire control radar on the heavily defended island. Von Sydow had elected to take the aircraft near the island to shorten the distance to the downed aviator.

Meanwhile, Jones and Cockerham asked permission to test their guns, and when granted found both guns promptly jammed. However, the spares worked as advertised. As they passed, Hon Mat Island Jones watched the area intensely for any flashes and was more than happy to see the gamble worked.

As BM 73 approached the area, Rooney heard a warbling sound from the survival radio beeper. Von Sydow was able to get an ADF (automatic directional finder) cut and saw Woolcock was south at 185 degrees. Only 22 minutes had transpired from the Mayday alert and locating the survivor.

In the cabin, Jones saw the destroyers blasting away, only to be answered by NVA near misses, white columns of water arriving near the tin cans. Shells were flying in both directions, and the helo flew under the arcs as it headed for the survivor.

In the distance, he could see the darkened hills of the coast. The sun had already set, and it was approaching darkness. The loss of visibility would not make the mission any easier. So, he searched for any boats heading to see and snatch their prize. However, either they weren't there or were concealed by the approaching night.

Powerhouse 305, having suffered battle damage and a leaking fuel, finally head to leave the scene, to be relieved by the remaining two Skyhawks of the flight. Rick St. Clair in Powerhouse 315 now gave the Big Mother a final vector.

Jones could see the coast from his gun mount and saw lights flashing along the beach line. It reminded him of the training flights from Ream Field and seeing car lights going to and from Coronado. However, reality quickly set in, and he knew these lights weren't heading to the marina but were gun flashes from enemy batteries interspersed with the explosions of five-inch shells shot from the destroyers. He began to pray quickly, "Lord let me be 20, Lord let me be 20." The next day, he would turn 20 years of age. It was a young man's war.

Lt. (jg) Rooney had a visual sighting of Woolcock bobbing in his raft and the HAC, Lt. von Sydow took control and put his bird in a hover near Woolcock. The '63 graduate of the Academy had flown as a co-pilot in the 66 cruise, and he now put all his experience and skill into the mission.

Since Woolcock was still in his raft, Jones made hands gestures from the cabin to get the downed pilot to abandon the raft, but to no avail. Just as the rotor wash from the helo began to blow the raft away, an enemy round landed a football field away. "Lord let me be 20."

Jones than directed his pilot to fly back over the survivor, dragging the rescue cable over him, which was successful. However, Woolcock still clung to the raft even when he was getting in the sling. Jones elected to hit the raise button on the hoist and jerk him out of the raft, but while this was transpiring, a second round hit an equal distance away and opposite from the first. Bracketed!!! "Lord let me be 20."

Lt. von Sydow's voice came clear on the intercom, "Come on boys, we got to go."

Jones heard no fear, but a need for expedience in his pilot's words.

Woolcock held on in a death grip as he was being hoisted from the water. As soon as he was clear, von Sydow broke hover, moving away from where the gunners had targeted. As Woolcock approached the cabin, he was impaired from entry by the gun mount, but after a few brief seconds of tugging by Cockerham, he was cleared and placed in the troop seat. Big Mother 73 broke for the Dewey. The NVA, a persistent lot, fired two SAM's at the departing helo. However, without a Fansong lock, they were shooting in the blind. The ECM operator aboard the Perth determined the helo and destroyers were being painted by a search radar with the NATO code of Cross Lot, allowing the battery commanders to have a rough bearing and distance to their targets. The SAM did present a sight for the retreating crew, streaking across the sky, trailing a white cloud, and when command detonated the 200-kilo warhead, exploding and igniting all the unused missile fuel. If it wasn't so deadly, it could have been a beautiful sight.

The crew quickly examined Woolcock. Then the reason he had refused to ditch his raft became apparent. His hand was torn open, the meaty part just below the thumb pushing out of the ripped skin. The crew remarked later that it looked like a bratwurst that had burst on the grill. With the waters known to be infested with Hammerhead Sharks it could be understood why he was reluctant on entering the water with night fast approaching.

Jones could briefly see both destroyers as they departed. Thank the lord for tin can sailors; they had diverted their fire from the batteries that were engaging them to the batteries that were firing at the Big Mother. Five-inch shells landed every few seconds, creating flashes that looked like cars on the Coronado highway. The gunners quickly took von Sydow's bird under their wing and protected it. These gunners and their quick and accurate fire preserved the lives of the crew of BM 73. Soon, they turned seaward, and the battle was concluded.

As von Sydow and Rooney headed to the Dewey, Jones and Cockerham performed first aid on Woolcock. Examining the wound, they applied a topical antiseptic and wrapped it in a battle dressing. In the medical kit was medicinal brandy. It was Coronet. To fortify Woolcock's spirits, he broke the seal and offered the pilot the mini bottle. Woolcock shook his head, and not wishing to be wasteful, Jones fortified his own spirit and cast the empty bottle out the cargo door.

Big Mother aircraft squeezed aboard a DLG landing deck. Forward of rotor blades was the aft missile mount. In the black of night with a rolling, pitching deck, combined with swirling winds eddying around the destroyer superstructure landings an adventure. Photo courtesy of Raunchy Redskins

As Big Mother approached the Dewey, another hazard emerged. Harbor Master II had directed the crew to land so the ship's doctor to examine the wound. However, the Dewey was not equipped with night landing lights. So, they would need a white-knuckle approach in the darkness. The Dewey turned thirty degrees starboard of the wind direction to get maximum wind across the deck in the direction the helo would approach. That move caused the ship to wallow in the waves. The ensuing wind flowing around the superstructure also buffeted the oncoming helo. Jim Rooney, with eyes on the rotor tips and the aft missile launcher of the Dewey, kept his HAC cleared forward. Jones, with gunners' belt snug, leaned as far as he could from the cargo door and insured the tail wheel cleared the deck aft. When he called, "Tail clear," von Sydow gingerly lowered the collective and put the 20,000-pound helo on the postage stamp. His skill won the day.

They were met by a corpsman, who whisked their still wet pilot to the sick bay. Big Mother crew still had their adrenaline flowing when they were ordered to stand by for flight operations. At 19:30, they were given the command to fly Woolcock to the Ranger for additional medical care.

The takeoff was not as thrilling as the earlier one that evening. However, it was still hazardous in the pitch-black night, and they were soon heading to Grey Eagle, the call sign of the U.S.S. Ranger (CVA-61). Landing on the super carrier was anticlimactic and Woolcock underwent a four-hour operation to repair his hand.

This rescue would herald the closing of a brief era of the squadron's history. It was the last CSAR mission flown by HS-6 in Vietnam. HC-7, which had started the CSAR business in the summer with the Clementine Detachments, was now assuming the place of Big Mother of the H-3 rescue roles within their detachment 110. They assumed H-3 duties on the 30th of January 1968. HC-7 received three experienced SAR crewmen (Nobles, Thomas, and Peters) TAD (temporary addition to duty) from HS-6 and additional personnel by transfer (Gonerka, Jones, and Williams).

For HS-6, new missions were on the horizon as the North Koreans had attacked the US Naval ship, U.S.S. Pueblo, killing one sailor and capturing the rest, along with the ship.

Notes:

November 1968 edition of Shipmate
Redlands Daily Facts, June 28, 1968, edition
Naval Aviation Squadron Lineages www.history.navy.mil
Wikpedia.org/wiki/USS Oriskany_(CVA34)
Rollingthunderremembered.com-11-january-1968
Phillips, T. Wings of Gold, 2008, Shootout in the Gulf
Rescue Recap Lt. Vernon Hans von Sydow January 1968
Pacific Stars and Stripes January 29, 1968, Sea Battle Rages During Rescue of Pilot
Conversations with Bob Westhorp, ECM operator on the RAN Perth D-38
Galdorisi, G. & Phillips, T. (2008) *Leave No Man Behind,* Zenith Press

CHAPTER 16

OPERATION FORMATION STAR

The Pueblo had begun its naval journey when it was launched in Kewaunee, Wisconsin in 1944. as a US Army freight vessel. The USN version was classified as an AKL, a light cargo ship, and was placed in reserve (aka the mothball fleet) at the conclusion of WW2. The Defense Department, searching for a vessel to gather radio and signal intelligence rescued it and placed it in service in 1964. In 1966, it was transferred to the US Navy, renamed the USS Pueblo, and given the hull designation of AGER 2.

Budgetary constraints postponed installing electronic intelligence equipment until 1967. Then the new commanding officer inspected the craft and promptly requested an engine overhaul, which was denied. He requested an emergency scuttling system for the ship, which was also denied. He requested demolition charges for emergency scuttling, also denied.

His request for a fuel fed document destruction incinerator was denied, although he purchased a lesser device using morale money. He requested that the ship's library of classified materials be reduced; that too was also denied.

The ship arrived at the Naval Station San Diego for its shakedown cruise in September of 1967. Upon reaching Japan, the skipper of the Naval Forces Japan directed the Pueblo to be armed with two M-2 .50 caliber machine guns. Lloyd Bucher, Pueblo's skipper, placed one on the bow and one on the stern. These guns were hidden under canvasses that would become frozen and stiff from the cold sea spray of the northern waters.

On the 11th of January 1968, the Pueblo left the naval base at Sasebo Japan, proceeded through the Tsushima Straits, and entered the Sea of Japan. Her mission, as a part of Operation Click-Beetle, was to conduct electronic surveillance of Soviet Naval activity in the area, while gathering radio intelligence of North Korea.

At the urgings of their Chinese ally, the North Korean People's Army had become more combative. In 1966, a total of 37 incidents were reported along the 38th parallel, the Korean DMZ. That total jumped to 435 with over 370 fatalities the following year.

The Korean peninsula became more intense on the 22nd when a North Korean assassination team attempted to kill South Korean President, Park Chung-hee in his residence, the Blue House. But the crew of the Pueblo was not apprised of this development. That same day, two fishing trawlers closed in to within 30 yards of the Pueblo. The crew designated them as Rice Paddy1 and Rice Paddy 2.

The following day, a submarine chaser of the Korean People's Navy challenged the Pueblo, to which Bucher responded by raising the Stars and Stripes. The United States recognized a twelve-mile limit to sovereignty whereas the Koreans maintained their national limits and extended it to fifty miles. As such, Bucher and his crew became caught in the middle. The Koreans ordered the Americans to stand down or be fired upon. Bucher attempted to maneuver the slow American ship away only to be deterred by warning shots. Additionally, a second subchaser and at least three torpedo boats now appeared on the scene. These were soon joined by several jets from the North Korean Air Force.

The Pueblo maintained radio communications with Naval Security in Japan, and Bucher was promised help, but it was not coming. The Fifth Air Force did not have any aircraft on immediate alert status and the closest Naval unit was the USS Enterprise some 500 miles away.

At first, the Koreans attempted to board the ship, but were thwarted when Bucher maneuvered the Pueblo away. The subchaser opened fire with its 57mm deck gun, while the torpedo boats closed in, firing their machine guns. The Pueblo's two .50 caliber machine guns were tucked away under frozen tarps. Their sailing orders included a paragraph instructing that all defensive armaments be hidden from view. The belts of ammunition were stowed below decks, and there was only one man in the crew with experience on the guns, a former army soldier who had reenlisted in the navy. All these factors made it difficult for the Pueblo to match the enemy fire.

When the North Koreans opened fire, the Pueblo crew began to dispose of classified materials. Though the shelling had forced the ship to halt, one of the sub chasers continued to fire, eventually killing Fireman Duane Hodges. Upon seeing this Bucher was forced to signal compliance and the Pueblo was boarded. The crew had their hands bound behind their backs, and soon felt the bayonets prodding into their bodies, as they were directed through the narrow passageways. They were blindfolded and beaten by the boarding parties from one of the sub chasers and a torpedo boat.

On the 28th of January, three days after HS-6 last combat rescue, a reconnaissance flight from Kadena AFB, confirmed the Pueblo was in North Korean custody in Wonsan Harbor.

Aboard the Kearsarge with the ASW air group, life seemed normal. However, Washington was a beehive. An American vessel had just been boarded and captured in international waters during a time of peace.

Soon, orders were being sent from the Pentagon, extending servicemen's enlistments. The scuttlebutt lawyers and rumor makers were having a field day as to what these developments would mean to the air groups and carrier battle groups throughout the navy.

Before forces were assembled, Congressional Washington was split on the appropriate response to make. Congressman Rivers suggested President Johnson give the North the option of releasing the ship and crew or face the nuclear wrath of the United States. But the American President was hesitant, as he did not wish to aggravate the situation and cause more harm to the crew. He decided to deploy military assets to the area while he began calling up reservists and extending the service time of others while flying regular reconnaissance flights over Wonsan. Then Operation Formation Star began one of the largest naval redeployments in modern history. With Vietnam going full throttle, some elements would need to be sent from the Gulf of Tonkin to the Sea of Japan. Six carrier battle groups would eventually be assembled to thwart the Korean threat.

Bucher and his crew were tortured daily. Their torture increased when their jailers discovered they were resisting subtly in the propaganda photos by extending their middle fingers in the international method of defiance. Bucher was consistently beaten and asked to confess, but he resisted all such notions until he was told that if he did not confess, his men would be executed one by one in front of him.

To prevent this, Bucher caved in. He wrote his confession carefully. "We paean the Democratic Republic of Korea and we paean their leader Kim il Sung". Then Bucher read his confession in front of the cameras as instructed and pronounced the word paean as "pee on".

Meanwhile, throughout the Pacific, Operation Formation Star began to assemble its assets. On the 25th of January, the USS Enterprise with Carrier Air Wing Nine, was directed to lead its battle group, with its screening cruisers and destroyers to Korean waters. Attached to the Enterprise was the USS Truxton (DLGN-35), USS Halsey (DLG-23), USS Ozbourn (DD-846), USS Collet (DD-730), USS O'Bannon (DDE-450), and the USS Higbee (DDR-806). The Enterprise Group was designated Task Force 70.6.

The Higbee would be remembered as the first American ship to be successfully bombed in Vietnam when an MIG-17 successfully placed a 250-kilogram bomb on its rear five-inch mount, destroying the mount. However, luck was with the Higbee crew as that mount had just suffered a hang fire and was cleared of personnel before being struck.

A few days later, Task Group 77.7 would be ordered to depart from North Vietnamese waters and head to Korean Waters. The USS Yorktown with an ASW group was ordered to join the Enterprise and Ranger groups. This new grouping was designated Task Force 71. The Yorktown's anti-submarine helos combined with the attached destroyers provided as screening force for sub surface craft, while its two squadrons of S2F aircraft provided airborne naval surveillance.

Eventually, TF 71 would have four attack carriers, (Enterprise, Ranger, Coral Sea, and Ticonderoga) with their Air Wings (9,2,15, and 19 respectfully). The Kearsarge and Yorktown with their Air Groups 53 and 55, would provide ASW, air surveillance, and logistical support. They also provided a CSAR asset, if needed. Additional ASW assets were provided by P-2 and P-3 long range Patrol Bombers from squadrons (VP-2, VP-17, VP-19, and VP-48.) Three of these squadrons were forward deployed to NAS Sangley Point, Philippines, and Marine Corps Air Station Iwakuni Japan.

At least six submarines joined the group, three older WW2 fleet boats, the Greenfish (SS-351), Segundo (SS-398), and the Volader (SS-400). With the fleet boats were two nuclear powered attack submarines the Swordfish (SSN-579), and the Flasher (SSN-613). The modern diesel electric Blueback (SS-581) was also dispatched.

It was tough sailing for the subs with sea ice adding to the hazards. The Swordfish sustained damage to its mast from ice. When the Swordfish sailed to Sasebo for repairs, Japanese newsmen asked about the damage, not wishing to disclose its original mission, the crew replied they had struck flotsam. However, the Soviets read the story and deduced that the Swordfish was the cause of one of their nuclear submarines being lost (K-129) in the Pacific. Two months after this incident, the USS Scorpion was lost with all hands.

The Segundo had a more daring mission. They were to travel under cover and submerge in Wonsan Harbor. The sub had five special operations men aboard. With a mission more suitable for a James Bond novel, they traveled submerged but were discovered by an ASW craft belonging to the North Korean Navy and were subjected to two days of depth charging. Machinist Mate Chief Russ Noragon recalled that they were desperately short of oxygen towards the end of their ordeal. "Most of the crew was suffering headaches from lack of oxygen." The chief noticed that code books and crypto gear were being assembled along with ballast, and he thought, "This isn't good." Finally, by launching decoys and diverting North Korean attention, the Segundo slipped away, though it suffered damage from the depth charging. It had one fuel cell ruptured, and many of its deck plates damaged by the overpressure caused by the underwater explosions.

Things were heating up on the Korean Peninsula.

To keep this growing Task Force supported, two oilers were dispatched, (the Platte and Tolavana), along with the Mars and Sacramento to provide combat support and ammunition.

HS-6 would turn over SAR duties to HC-7 Det 110 on the 18th of February 1968 in a ceremony held on the hanger deck of the Kearsarge. Prior to that moment three of the crewmen of HS-6, Nobles, Peters, and Thomas) had volunteered to remain on SAR duty with HC 7 on a temporary basis (TAD), allowing the new squadron time to gather and train a new cadre of H-3 crewmen. The following day, the Kearsarge left Yankee Station to join the Task Force near Korea.

When the Kearsarge and its escorts arrived, the first thing the crews noticed was that they were not in the tropics anymore. The helos still had the gun mounts which facilitated a large hole forward where the entrance ladder/door once stood. The freezing temperatures became more pronounced with flow-through ventilation entering the cabin at 100 mph. Seeing this, the anti-exposure suits were broken out of storage, and used to provide protection for the parts of the body that was covered, the hands and face were still exposed to the elements.

The crew made numerous passes by the ever-growing number of Soviet surface ships in the area. The first crewmen had the pleasure of opening the cargo door and using the so-called Mark 1 BAC (Big A^^ Camera) would photograph the Soviets, focusing on radar antennae, radio equipment, armament and disregarding the Soviets on deck with pants down and allowing the moon to shine. More than one crewman extended their middle finger in the universally accepted token of love and respect.

The days that followed could be described as a heroic monotonous toil for the squadron, comprising logistic flights, photo reconnaissance, endlessly boring holes into a cold sky, while blowing on hands and fingers to restore a semblance of warmth. Although it was not a topic of discussion among many of the crews, an impending CSAR possibility loomed on the horizon as more and more of the Task Force arrived on station.

Unknown to the crews of HS-6, the staffs of the American and South Korean militaries were preparing to launch alpha strikes against the ten known North Korean air bases in suppression raids to facilitate the rescue of the Pueblo and her crew. At the time of the seizure, the DPRK Air Force fielded some 657 aircraft, with most of the fighter aircraft of the older MIG 15 or MIG 17 variety. Although ten newer MIG 21 aircraft were counted on the runways. A month later, with escalation of the situation a distinct possibility, only 279 aircraft remained. The rest sought safer pastures across the Yalu on Chinese airfields.

Despite the obvious advantages, this show of strength was having an impact on the Navy's resources.

The Siege of Khe Sanh had begun just days prior to the Pueblo's capture. At the end of January, the North Vietnamese launched the Tet Offensive, bringing the forces of the South and their allies under fire throughout the country. Admiral Moorer then advised that Operation Formation Star could only endure for a maximum of six weeks before the USN air operations in Vietnam would be seriously impacted.

The flip side of the coin was that reducing Task Force 71 would hamper the US efforts at Panmunjom, the site of the Pueblo negotiations with North Korea. The US Ambassador to the South had sent a message to Washington advising against pulling TF 71 from the area, " withdrawal of the carriers will not advance matters and probably retard progress…"

In the end, President Johnson decided to pursue a diplomatic end. Eventually, after daily bouts of torture and abuse, the 83 Americans were released. The event did not go unnoticed in Naval circles. Many officers, senior petty officers in wardrooms, ready rooms, chiefs' messes, and galleys were left with the memory that an American ship was attacked, boarded, crewman killed, and others captured while the perpetrator maintained impunity. The limitations of power were clear. The Mayaguez Incident a few years later would mitigate this to a degree, but not erase it totally.

With Operation Formation Star ending, the Kearsarge was released from Defender Station in the Korean Waters March 22. 1968. For HS-6 pilots, crew, and maintenance men this Westpac was ending, and they would soon be sailing, with stops in Japan and Hawaii, to the friendly confines of NAS Imperial Beach.

Notes:
Navcource.org Pueblo Incident: Two Failed Submarine Missions by Bill Sreifer
Conversations with Captain Rick Grant (Ret)

Conversations with Captain William Nyborg (Captain USS Kearsarge) to Terry Hall at Kearsarge Reunion

Mobley, R. Lessons From the Capture of the USS Pueblo and the Shootdown of a US Navy EC 121

Bucher, Lloyd, *Bucher My Story* Doubleday & Company ISBN 0385072449

Prados, John The Navy's Biggest Betrayal archived on the Wayback Machine 17 Nov 2015

CHAPTER 17

HS-6 CREWMEN SHINE IN HC-7

Three HS-6 aircrew volunteered for a temporary-addition-to-duty assignment with the Sea Devils of HC-7. These three, Alan Nobles, Chris Thomas, and Bob Peters had departed the squadron prior to the Pueblo's seizure. Three more, Leonard Gonerka, Rick Williams, and Johnny Jones were transferred on a permanent basis; Gonerka prior to the Pueblo capture and the other two in March.

The first change the transferring crewmen noticed was a difference in philosophy in the rescue techniques. The Sea Devils, morphing from HC 1, demanded more specific training for the rescue crewmen, whereas in the HS squadrons the primary focus was antisubmarine warfare, and detecting and tracking submarines with a dipping sonar transducer lowered hundreds of feet below the helo.

The incoming crewmen were assigned temporarily to Pararescue Team 1 in Cubi Point.

The enlisted petty officer in charge of training was a Hospital Corpsman Petty Officer 2nd Class Bliss.

Bliss and his crew would begin training at 0600. Training would start with a five-mile run through the Zambales Mountains, and the trainees being released for breakfast afterwards. At 0800, pool swims would commence with instruction in different strokes for speed and endurance. By 0900, the initiates would be swimming with a M14 rifle attached to their neck, pulling their head under water, and making breathing an event of labor, while familiarizing the students with the prospect of handling stressful situations in water. Later in the morning, the rifles were exchanged for packs filled with 45 pounds of rocks, again putting the students in stressful water situations. At 1200 hours, they were released for lunch and would reconvene at 1300 hours for classroom instruction on the different parachutes used by the various air forces in theatre (US, South Vietnamese, Australian, etc.) and the release mechanism in each. On some days, this was followed by techniques in clearing chute tangles in the most expeditious manner. On other days, they would practice water entries from a helicopter moving at 10 knots and 10 feet while wearing masks and fins. When the course was nearing its end, water entry would begin a multi-mile ocean swim in Subic Bay, accompanied by small boats carrying rifle equipped sailors on shark patrol. Only after passing the Pararescue Course would the crewmen be released to the detachments. For the H-3 crewmen, Detachment 110 awaited.

For the author, the hardest day with Pararescue 1 was the second day, Tuesday. At the conclusion of Day 1, Bliss's minions, two third class petty officers invited the class to the local watering hole in Olongapo, the city adjacent to the sprawling US Naval complex. Once there, the students were invited and encouraged to celebrate their training with copious amounts of San Miguel beer accompanied by the local gin. The gin was of the highest quality. If one shopped carefully in the various sari-sari stores surrounding the base, he would find that a liter of the perilous spirit would cost the equivalent of one US dollar. This, the instructors called, the "wetting in" ceremony. The following morning, during the five-mile run through the Zambales mountains, occurred what the Para Rescue 1 team called the "puking in" ceremony, accompanied by catcalls and laughter from the members of Para 1. Graduation would be accompanied by another trip to Olongapo and the obligatory rounds of San Miguel.

Upon reaching the Gulf, things got serious in a hurry. Gonerka was the first of the HS-6 crew to experience action, as he had PCS (Permanent Change of Station) orders to HC-7.

On February 23, 1968, Gonerka was crewed with pilot, Lt. Barie Snider, co-pilot Ens. Byron Dieckman, and crewman AE-2 Raymond Harvey. As they awaited the call, Major Laird Gutterson and his weapons officer, 1st Lt. Myron Donald were flying combat air patrol approximately fifty miles north of Haiphong when they were jumped by North Vietnamese MIG 21's. Their F-4, call sign Honda 04, was soon struck with an atoll, Soviet made air to air missile.

For Gutterson, this had to be déjà vu In December he was attacking a ferry near Dong Ha when his F-4 was hit and he sought the closest safe zone, feet wet in the Gulf where he was plucked from the water by the Big Mothers. Flying in the 497th Tactical Fighter Squadron was not for the faint of heart.

This time he would not be so lucky. He and his back seater were forced to call Mayday, eject, and hit the silk ten miles before they reached the shoreline.

Snider and the crew of Big Mother 70 were prepositioned on the North SAR ship, the USS Halsey, and were scrambled to the SAR alert. They quickly approached the coast only to be recalled to a safer distance for Harbor Master to organize a rescue operation. They returned to the Halsey but was launched again, only to be recalled again. The third time, Snider was advised they would be going in high with RESCAP above them. Snider would need to stay under 10,000 feet in the helo as they were not equipped with oxygen.

The co-pilot, Dieckman, later wrote to the HC-7 historian, "The call came in early in the day and we got our info grabbed, our gear, briefed and launched, but got most of the way to feet dry and then got recalled. We launched again and got recalled a second time…evidently the powers that be wanted to "get organized". After a lengthy delay we were asked if we would go in "high" with the jet escorts. With no O2, we were limited to 10K', but that made them feel better as weather was very, very poor. They said they would escort us (well, many thousands of feet above us) and they would have us descend in a spiral about 9K' in the goo to break out in a valley with the tops of the hills clear of clouds. I believe we refueled on the USS Halsey, then proceeded. Naturally the IFR transit was a pucker, the descent was a pucker and when we broke out of the clouds, the clouds were not clear of the tops of the hills and at the altitude we were flying…a few hundred feet at best, we were often not in contact with the beeper. We crossed from valley to valley at the notches where visibility would permit, and eventually picked up the beeper again. After making every effort over a substantial period to close on the signal we were informed that the jets (many thousands of feet overhead) were now low on fuel, oh, and by the way Migs were launching (probably from the Hanoi area) and they wanted us to come out. Dang! It's not like the jets were doing us any good as it was.

We asked for pigeons (a direction to exit to the coast), and we received a heading which we expected to be one thoughtfully considered. We flew that nominal heading, still going from one saddle back to another to remain VFR and hopefully discourage the Mig's from joining us. We crossed a ridgeline at a saddle back and surprisingly the whole valley was open under a smooth-domed overcast, and we were over a large city/town. As we evaluated the scene (only a few seconds), flak opened up around us everywhere, so Barie Snider, the Aircraft Commander did a quick-stop and a spiral to the deck, and we proceeded as fast as the helo could fly right down the center of town right at rooftop level. People were shooting at us from various parts of town with machine gun fire being obvious because of the tracers, soldiers were jumping out of trucks and shooting at us with small arms. Of course, we were doing our fair share of shooting as well. I know the crew (Petty Officers Harvey and Gonerka) was making a hell of a racket, I managed to get a double-taped clip emptied, then considered and readied the grenade launcher but no suitable target seemed worthwhile. Unreal, not frightening, just unreal and tense. I would have sworn we were hit more than we were, but evidence showed otherwise. There was damage; a hydraulic leak obviously pouring from the hydraulics closet, possibly from weapons fire, and the concern was getting somewhere while we still had control. We made it to the beach and moved out into an area of offshore Karst formations that today are a big tourist/cruise ship draw of Ha Long Bay. I always thought we exited close to Cam Pha, but it may have been closer to Haiphong looking at the bay formations. Map consultations were not the priority at that moment…we were where we were. As we approached the beach fire abated somewhat. Beautiful scenery…just amazing. The

Karst, beautiful beach, junks with red/brown sails, clear water. That notwithstanding, the aircrew still had things to shoot at occasionally. We passed a long thin canoe type vessel with one old man in it, and I was amazed that PO Harvey opened fire, ineffectively thank goodness, and I called for him to cease, at about the same time the old man did a dive into the water. As we continued offshore the coastal defense sites opened on us and we started serious jinking as the water plumes burst about us. Close but not so close that we got wet. Once clear our only goal was to get to the USS Halsey. It wasn't Baries' best landing, but it was effective, I think I'll give him credit for doing well with a degraded hydraulic system," he joked.

And thus ended HC-7s first Detachment 110 rescue attempt. They had inherited the role from HS 6 and gave it their best shot on the first call. The weather, lack of radio contact with downed crew, MIG alerts, coupled with the removed RESCAP cover had all contributed to this crew being ordered out by rescue command. A less than thought out pigeons command had placed them over a populated city, where ground fire could be expected. So, they nursed their injured bird back to the Halsey. Post flight examinations showed they had suffered flak damage to the rotor blades and had been penetrated by ground fire in the cabin. However, no crewmen had been hit. For the HS-6 transferee, Gonerka, he had performed at a very high level.

On April 15, 1968, tax day in the States, parachutes began to rain from the sky near Vinh, North Vietnam as two Phantoms from Fighter Squadron 114 (The Fighting Aardvarks) had endured a midair collision and the four crewmen were forced to eject.

At 15:22, the Big Mother crew of Lt (jg) Donald Nicholson, Ens. Jeff Wiant, AX-3 Bob Peters, and ADJ-3 Jeffrey English received the alert and were aloft at 15:27. As soon as Big Mother 72 left the Halsey, the Clementine crew began to unfold the UH-2 stored aboard and make it ready for flight. Soon, both Sea Devil crews were in the air and heading into harm's way.

Nicholson and the Big Mother crew received a vector that took them eighteen miles south of Vinh, near the Song Cua Sot River. The crew began to take fire as they crossed into feet dry territory. A few clicks inland they received new coordinates and did a 180-degree turn, reengaging the fire that greeted them just minutes before. As they approached the area where the river met the gulf, they could see men in the water. Wiant kept the men in visual sight as Nicholson closed the distance. The Clementine aircraft was now approaching the scene, evading the incoming shells fired from a nearby hill.

Big Mother, traveling west, and steered to the right, as they moved near the downed airmen. The helo descended to ten feet, then slowed to ten knots, as the command ten and ten was passed to Peters, who gave English the triple tap on shoulder after seeing no debris in the water below. English, exiting the helo, rotated his body to face the wind. Holding his mask in place with his left hand, he extended his right arm across his chest to keep the force of the water from pushing his rescue gear against his face.

Upon entering the water, he saw his helo fly away, taking the ground fire with it. The Clementine aircraft was also doing the same thing. Nicholson and Wiant directed Peters to toss smoke markers when they were away from the downed aviators, to confuse the gunners, and give them false targets.

After throwing the smoke markers, Peters grabbed the hoist hook and unwound an amount of hoist cable sufficient to reach the water. Then he wound the cable into a large coil. He hooked the horse collar with only one end attached to the hook so when he tossed it to English, it would be easier to grab, faster to attach, and its buoyancy would keep the hook above water. When the helo approached the downed pilot and swimmer, Peters tossed the cable, therefore saving time in hover by not waiting for the hoist to unwind. English grabbed the collar, attached it to the pilot, attached himself by his swimmer d-ring, and signaled Peters to hoist. As soon as they broke water, Peters relayed this information to the cockpit, and Nicholson broke hover. Wiant tossed another smoke marker to give the gunners ashore one more dummy target. English, attached to the rescue hoist with the downed F-4 crewman, was trailing behind the helo in the wind stream, akin to a fisherman trolling for his catch. However, once aboard, he prepared for his next adventure.

As Nicholson's crew completed the first rescue, Clementine 2 was also finished with their first pickup of the day, as both crews repeated their procedures and began to extricate the final two crewmen. The second rescue was aided by a flight of Skyhawks that arrived as RESCAP. In a few minutes, it was rinsed, repeated, and the Sea Devils returned the four Fighting Aardvarks to their squadron. It was almost routine, except for the groundfire, NVA artillery bombarding the rescue area, and waters filled with hammerheads and venomous sea snakes. But for these occurrences, it was just another day at work: punch the clock, go home, and take four crewmen from the jaws of capture or death with you. In this vein, Peters had represented both squadrons well.

After the rescue mission, the Commanding Officer of the Air Wing sent the following message, "Hawk, COMCVW-11 and all our pilots wish to express highest admiration and appreciation for superb rescue of four VF-114 aircrewmen in the afternoon of 15 April. Instantaneous aggressive response and smooth coordination are comforting proof of truly professional SAR Team on Yankee Station. The great courage and can-do spirit of Big Mother 71 and Clementine 2 crews in the face of intense enemy fire commands greatest respect and admiration of aviators on scene. Will provide supporting verification for any contemplated citation if desired. LCDR FARNSWORTH, LTJGs SARNECKY, MCCREADY, BAER convey their personal thanks." The CSAR efforts were greatly appreciated by those that flew into the jaws of Hell every day.

* * *

A few weeks later, on the 7th of May, another Phantom from the Enterprises Fighting 92nd squadron, also known as the Silver

Wings, found itself in trouble. The phantom, Silver Kite 210, was itself in a tight spot after engaging in a dogfight with several MIG 21s near Vinh. Lcdr Ejnar Christianson and his back seater, Lt (jg) Worth Kramer were running low on fuel and needed to head back to the carrier when they were struck by an Atoll missile fired by one of the Migs. He was flying at 8,000 feet when it hit and managed to clear the coast before his craft burst into flames and began to spiral out of control. Christianson and Kramer both successfully ejected, landing a few miles from the coast.

Aboard the USS Jouett, a DLG on South SAR duty, was the crew of Tex Wiley, Ens. Richard Everett, ATN2 Leonard Gonerka, and AX3 James Lawrence. The CIC of the Jouett, having been alerted to the Mayday call, announced SAR Alert, and the crew of the Big Mother 71 scurried to their aircraft. They had been alerted at 15:34, and were crewed and ready to launch immediately, although they shut down for a few moments to await confirmation of SAR mission. However, they were airborne, and heading to the downed pilots within six minutes of the first alert.

At 15:56, the survivors released a smoke flare which was seen by the inbound rescue crew. Using the Sea Devils ten and ten method, Lawrence, the swimmer, dove into the water. He located one of the downed pilots, secured him with the collar, attached his d-ring to the hook, and signaled Gonerka. They were quickly hoisted aboard. One down, one to go.

However, the second rescue would be more problematic, as the shore batteries began to bracket the BM 71. Quickly, the Phantoms from the downed crew squadron were joined by two aircraft from the Ticonderoga and attempted to suppress the increasing fire from the coast, while Silver Kites 204 and 215 made strafing runs on nearby junks that were nearing the rescue scene.

During this melee, the Big Mother throttle on number two engine vibrated loose, forcing the co-pilot, Ens. Everett to concentrate on the engine settings and power. As such, Tex Wiley had to monitor the shore bombardment, fly the bird, and do the maneuvers to facilitate a ten and ten approach. The hoist threw another wrench into the mixture, as it began to perform sluggishly. As Lawrence and the Phantom crewmen were being hoisted to the door, the Dutch type M-60 mount vibrated loose, impairing Gonerka's access to the two men in the hoist. However, with some difficulty, they were able to bring both men into the cabin. Then Wiley had Big Mother exited the scene. Upon their return, the crew received a hearty message of congratulations from RADM Epps, "The bold and prompt rescue under fire of the crew of Silver Kite 210 near enemy territory was another vivid example of the bravery and skill of our SAR helo crews and the professionalism of all the forces supporting their efforts. Well Done to all concerned and especially to the crew of Big Mother 71. I convey the deep appreciation and admiration of all CVA airmen for your selfless dedication to their safety.

A special Kudo also to the instant RESCAP, Silver Kites 204/215 from Enterprise and Feed-Bass 110/112 from Ticonderoga whose timely help with suppressive fire made the rescue possible…"

The next day, the HS-6 transferees would be called upon again. This time, the Big Mothers were crewed by Lt Gary McConnell, Lt (jg) John Nichols, crew of Alan Nobles and John Cullivan. The crew had an uneventful morning before getting the call for help.

A flight of A-4 Skyhawks from the Enterprise's Attack Squadron 56 was conducting an armed reconnaissance mission near the area of Ha Tinh. Lt. Lawrence had rolled in on a column of trucks and fired his rockets at the target, rolled out, and was climbing when he was struck by ground fire. He noticed an increasing vibration in the engine, which was quickly followed by a fire warning light as his aircraft began to burn. He later stated that he knew he couldn't make the coast and turned back towards the mountains to provide better cover. Soon, the engine seized, forcing Lawrence to eject. As he drifted to earth, he knew he was nearly 20 miles from the coast.

Big Mother 70 received the SAR Alert at 12:06 from Lawrence's wingman who had remained in the area. The helo was 50 miles from the scene. Nobles recalled, "we proceeded until feet dry to the area where we believed the pilot to be…I remember a lot of radio chatter from RESCAP while we scanned the very deep and thick jungle below…the downed pilot radioed he could hear us and we were getting closer and closer…we slowed almost to a hover, than all hell broke loose, the pilot said we were taking fire from the right side of the aircraft and I began to lay down suppressive fire. The pilot said the casings were dropping on him, and that indicated he was directly below us." The helo did not have a jungle penetrator (a rescue device that could penetrate the foliage, then fold out a seat like apparatus for the downed pilot to ride up) on board, so the crew improvised and hooked a tie down chain to the hoist and collar and let the weight break through the foliage.

Lt. Lawrence had a different view, a much closer view of the events that were unfolding. When his chute opened, he was only 200 feet above the jungle canopy. The proximity to the jungle canopy caused his chute to become entangled in a tree, leaving him dangling five to six feet above the jungle floor. He released himself, falling into a mud bank alongside a steep hill. Then he slid down the bank.

Once he regained his footing, he started up the hill and halted when he heard a noise. Slowly, he began to climb and finally got a glimpse of the source of the noise. There was a Vietnamese man, wearing shorts and a sleeveless blue shirt, armed with a machete. It appeared to Lawrence that he was trying to cut his way down to the crash site. He waited a few moments until the Vietnamese was out of sight and began to follow a dry creek bank. Prior to reaching the top of the hill, Lawrence came upon a clearing with a small lean-to shack, and a cluster of coals from a fire., and wondered if this belonged to the machete swinging man he had seen earlier.

Due to the jungle cover, Lawrence could hear aircraft overhead but could not see them. He continued to forge his way through until he finally saw rays of sunshine ahead, and a clearing, perhaps 15 feet across, emerged. At that point, the exhausted Lawrence sat down, put his back against the closest tree, and brought out his radio. But he was far from being safe. He could hear search parties approaching him. They weren't quiet. They didn't need to be. They were the hunters, and he was their prey.

He told himself that this was ground zero. He could either be captured there or be found by the rescue forces. However, the din of the closing search parties told him he would be more likely to face the former than the latter. There was no other way. The Vietnamese communicated among themselves by making whistling calls to each other, and they were closing in fast. He said later that at that moment he thought, "Oh God, I have had it."

Then, a few minutes later, he heard a helo approaching. He got a glimpse of the long shadow it made moving over the trees and knew it was a Big Mother. He screamed into his survival radio that the helo was passing over him. As it passed, he could hear automatic weapons firing from the crest of the hill. The Vietnamese had begun turning up the heat on his rescuers.

When the helo made its second pass, Lawrence keyed his mike and asked if they had a visual sighting of him. He saw the pilot nod that he did. As McConnell brought Big Mother into a hover, Lawrence heard shouting in Vietnamese as their troops amplified their fire on the helo. Lawrence keyed his mike and told McConnell to spray the area and was soon rewarded with empty brass casings and links falling on his position as Cullivan and Nobles used their two M-60s to lay suppressing fire on the jungles surrounding the clearing.

Soon, he saw the hoist with the tie down chain attached appear through the canopy. It was getting caught on tree branches, and Lawrence had to wrench it off, dropping his radio in the process. It was not until he hooked himself to the hoist and could not signal the helo to hoist that he knew something was wrong. Looking around, he spied his survival radio six feet away, quickly retrieved it and transmitted for the helo to hoist. But there was no reply from the hoist operator. Lawrence continued to give the call to hoist, and after a short period of time, discovered that he was the one at fault. In his excitement, he had been pushing the receive button instead of the transmit. He corrected the error immediately and was soon lifted from the floor of the jungle.

Once he cleared the trees, he could hear heavy firing all around him. The air was thick with incoming rounds. He later reported, "I was just cringing, waiting for the bullet to come plowing into me." As Cullivan hoisted him into the cabin, Nobles continued to lay down heavy suppressing fire from his M-60. When he saw that Lawrence had cleared the canopy, he told the flight station to get out of the area.

The rest of the rescue was quite normal, as normal as flying to the coast in a loud slow helo over enemy territory, while everyone and his brother tried to take a shot at you could be. Lawrence was flown back to his carrier to the greetings of his squadron. He took a moment to mug for the camera by hugging the horse collar hanging from the hoist in front of Cullivan's gun position and gave a huge smile demonstrating the relative safety of his environment.

Lawrence hanging from hoist aboard his carrier. Alan Nobles with back to camera. Photo courtesy Raunchy Redskins HS-6 website. Ken Burns

Admiral Eps sent the following: "For the second time in two days our SAR forces have successfully rescued a downed aircrew under hostile fire. The recovery of the pilot of Champion 406 from deep within enemy territory in an unbelievable short time was the result of the prompt, cool, and professional actions of the on-scene commander, the RESCAP, the downed pilot, and most of all the intrepid crew of Big Mother 70. You have the admiration and appreciation of all for scoring on this tough one. Well Done Admiral Horace Eps."

Notes:
Declassified Message from CO Air Wing 11 to CO HC 7, from HC-7 website, Ron Milam Historian
Galdorisi, G. & Phillips, T. (2008) *Leave No Man Behind,* Zenith Press
Phillips, T. *Cocked and Ready-Folded and Stuffed…and the Ten-and-Ten Maneuver,* Wings of Gold Fall 2013,
HC-7 The Sea Devils website Ron Milam historian
Email from Byron Dieckman to Ron Milam
Email from Alan Nobles to Ron Milam 1-27-2011

CHAPTER 18

HS-6 CREW CLOSEOUT THEIR DUTIES WITH THE SEA DEVILS

On the 21st of May, a flight of A-4 Skyhawks from Attack Squadron 93, also called the Blue Blazers, were attacking a bridge north of Vinh when another flight from the Bon Homme Richard (CVA-31) began to take fire from automatic weapons defending the bridge. Raven 313, flown by Lt (jg) Jack Douglas, realized he had been hit in the fuselage when his fellow pilots noticed flames coming from there. He immediately attempted to gain altitude and headed to the gulf. However, his control surfaces began to stiffen, and soon he lost all hydraulic power. As his aircraft became uncontrollable, he had no choice but to call Mayday and eject.

Big Mother, flying from the South SAR station of the USS Halsey (DLG-23), was making its racetrack pattern off the coast, a development also known as boring holes into the sky, when it received the Mayday call on the guard channel of 243 MHz at 16:40 in the afternoon. The crew consisted of Lt (jg) Michael White, Ens. Byron Dieckman, 1st crew AX3 Chris Thomas, and 2nd crew AE2 Bobby Childress. The Halsey gave Big Mother the vector and estimated the distance at 26 miles. Eleven minutes later, they were on the scene and had spotted the survivor in his survival raft, well clear of the chute.

The ten and ten maneuver was utilized, placing the swimmer in the water, where he then secured the survivor and was promptly hoisted aboard. Apart from the Dutch door M-60 mount making it difficult to get the survivor in the cabin, and the hoist ICS station faltering and growing intermittent, the operation was a smooth one. The entire rescue had been performed in two minutes from arrival to departure. Textbook work. At 17:09, Lt (jg) Douglas was aboard the Halsey, twenty-nine minutes after he called Mayday. A few minutes later, he was back aboard the Big Mother and on his way to his home away from home, the Bon Homme Richard, aka the Bonnie Dick to its airwing.

Douglas remarked, "In less than an hour, just as advertised, I can't say enough for the ejection and the rescue team." For the Sea Devils, he would be rescue number 38 in their brief existence to date.

* * *

On the 30th of May, Memorial Day in the States, Tex Wiley's crew of Dieckman, Gonerka, and Lawrence were the South SAR aircraft aboard the Halsey. At 10:07, a Mayday alert was heard from the guard frequency and the Harbor Master aboard the Halsey was notified.

Lt. James Killen, an A-4 Skyhawk pilot from Attack Squadron 212, aka the Rampant Raiders flying from the Bon Homme Richard, was making passes at targets, unloading his 2.75-inch ordinance on an oil storage facility north of Vinh. Somedays you do everything right and still the fates go against you. After his fifth firing pass, his engine ingested debris from the LAU-60 rocket pod and he immediately began to lose power.

Big Mother 71, sitting on a DLG at South Sar Station. This aircraft still carries HS-6 markings but was transferred to HC-7 when Det 110 assumed CSAR duties. The H-3 was a very large helo for a very small deck. Photo courtesy HS-6 Raunchy Redskins

Meanwhile, Tex Wiley's crew flying in Big Mother 71 had been in the air for an hour, making racetracks near the exit point of the day's air strikes.

Already losing power, altitude, and airspeed, Lt. Killan headed for the coast. A flying maxim has it could prove harmful to one's health if you lost altitude, airspeed, and ideas. Killan was losing the first two, but he was intent on keeping control of the last. It was time to hit the silk. He ejected a few miles North of Hon Mat Island, known to house assets of the North Vietnamese Army. It was not ideal, but he was out of options.

Wiley and the crew of Big Mother 71 were close enough when Killan ejected and watched him descend until splashdown. Then Wiley closed in on the spot, intent on executing a ten and ten approach. Having a faulty radar altimeter meant that his swimmer jumped from a higher altitude than anticipated, but Bliss and his minions had also had some of the trainees go at twenty and twenty. So, Lawrence, the swimmer, entered the water without incident, and immediately checked Killan for parachute entanglement before getting them ready to be hoisted aboard.

Though Gonerka experienced problems with the hoist, and needed to use manual mode, he was able to get Lawrence and Killan aboard. Then they proceeded toward the Halsey without further incident. Rescue number 40 was now in the books for the Sea Devils. However, it was not time to rest on their laurels.

* * *

Five days later on June 4th, a Phantom F-4J, flown by Lt. Eric Brice, was attacking road infrastructure south of Vinh by dropping Mk 82 five-hundred-pound bombs on the target. He had just made a pass and was climbing away from the target when the aircraft was hit by 37mm anti- aircraft fire at almost 4,500 feet. Brice immediately noticed that he had suffered hydraulic damage and had only his rudder for control. As if that was not enough, his throttle was also stuck on full military power.

Brice used all his skill to coax the stricken and badly damaged craft to the coast and into the Gulf. There, he was forced to leave the aircraft before events went catastrophic. The stuck throttle meant he was flying faster than ideal, but his options were fading fast. So, he ordered his back seater, Lt. William Simmons to eject. Simmons pulled his face curtain, separating his canopy, and the Martin-Baker system fired. However, the wind stream was so violent due to the craft's speed, when he ejected, the force of the wind broke an arm and a leg.

Simmons entered the water painfully and quickly became entangled with the parachute cords connecting his harness to the nylon canopy, and his injuries prevented him from clearing the entanglement.

Wiley and his crew had been on the USS Jouett, when the SAR Alert was sounded. They were aloft in five minutes and Wiley and Dieckman kept in constant contact with Brice's wingman, who was now orbiting the rescue area. Eight minutes after launch, the wingman had the helo in sight and vectored the Big Mother to Simmons. Simmons, on the other hand, was able to use his good arm to get a day marker smoke from his survival vest and activate it for the helo to obtain surface wind conditions and maintain visual on him.

The swimmer, Lawrence, utilizing the ten and ten, entered the water and soon had Simmons clear of the parachute cord. He then prepared for Simmons to be hoisted aboard. Twelve minutes from launch, Simmons was successfully aboard the Big Mother and inbound to the Jouett.

The celebrations for rescue number 41 were muted as the pilot, Brice, never cleared the aircraft and was last seen pounding on his stuck canopy. Without the canopy releasing the ejection sequence could not be completed. He was forced to ride his stricken aircraft into the gulf and was listed as KIA. Fighter Squadron 33 would only get one of their crew back. Twenty-five-year-old Brice was the first fatality in the 1968 cruise for the USS America, his parent carrier.

* * *

One week later, the 11th of June, Tex Wiley and crew were serving as SAR standby on the USS Yorktown when at 02:55 in the morning they were alerted by the ships 1MC that they would be launched to support the efforts of a search for a downed A-7 pilot Lcdr Randolph Ford and a flight of Corsairs from Attack Squadron 86 on a road reconnaissance mission. Ford had delivered a flare to let his wingman get a visual of any road traffic below them. The wingman did not see Ford get hit but saw a huge fireball below him and heard Lcdr Ford on his survival radio. The pilot was in his parachute but had sustained serious injuries during the ejection sequence.

Tex Wiley and crew, with Lt (jg) Gring flying as co-pilot, soon crossed the beach and were feet dry searching for the downed aviator. The area was flat and sandy with one solitary hill, and villages lay to the west and south of the search area. Closer to the beach was a line of trees, from which the Big Mother 71 began receiving heavy fire. Lawrence manned the starboard gun, while Gonerka positioned himself at the cargo door, and both began sweeping the area with suppressing fire.

But the small arms fire from the enemy only continued to grow. Here, a peculiar problem presented itself. The gunners M-60 rested on thin armor plate; the forward mount was a fixed mount, while the cargo mount was a Dutch door that could swing away. So, while Gonerka engaged the enemy, the flooring of the helo collecting the spent brass and links, a Kalashnikov round hit his mount straight on, passing through the armor plate, and the muscles on his calf. Luckily, no bone was struck but the run of luck ended there. The piece of armor plate that was dislodged by the 7.62 round entered the other leg. Thus, the enemy had scored a two for the price of one hit on the experienced crewmen.

Gonerka was one of the larger-than-life guys that our two squadrons had produced. When he was in HS-6, it was rumored that he had gone to personnel to change his name. When asked why he legally wished to change his name, he replied, "The name of Gonerka is of Polish-Jewish heritage, I do not want to be type cast as a Polish Jew, I want just your average All American boy name, something that fits in and goes unnoticed."

When asked what he would like his new name to be, he replied, "Hymie Irving Schwartz." Then the personnel man knew he was the victim of Gonerka's humor.

Gonerka had been brought back to the carrier for medical treatment, where it was decided he would need to be transferred to a hospital. He was on the flight deck, lying in a stokes litter, when the Admiral came by and shook his hand and asked if there was anything the admiral could do for him. Gonerka replied, "A beautiful blonde and a bottle of scotch would improve my morale."

The admiral replied, "Son, I think that request is beyond what I can do." However, legend has it that when Gonerka was aboard the helo transporting him to the hospital in Danang, a bottle of Scotch was lying in the stokes litter. He was on his own for female companionship.

For Gonerka, he had flown his last mission. He would be transferred to Danang, and then Japan for hospital duty and physical therapy prior to being discharged at the end of his enlistment.

HS-6 personnel with HC-7 had acquitted themselves well. In just a few months, they had contributed to five rescues and made two memorable attempts.

A more comprehensive list of HC-7 Sea Devil rescues and attempts will be contained in ***The Sea Devils, Sagas of Courage*** to be published in the second half of 2023.

Notes:
HC-7seadevils.org Ron Milam historian
Virtualwall.org/db/BriceEPO1a.htm
Memories of author while serving with
Leonard Gonerka

CHAPTER 19

THE FRANK E EVANS INCIDENT

The HC-7 became the primary SAR service in the Gulf of Tonkin when HS-6 returned to the Western Pacific in 1969. As such, their role became as arduous as it was before the 1966 logistics and ASW.

During the cruise, the Kearsarge Battle Group was sent several hundred miles southeast of Saigon (now Ho Chi Minh City) to participate in a joint allied naval training exercise. Joining the Kearsarge was the Her Majesties Australian Ship Melbourne, a Majestic class light carrier that had been laid down in WW2.

The Melbourne had been involved in a collision with the Australian destroyer Voyager, resulting in the loss of that destroyer and 82 of her crew. Though the Melbourne had been cleared of any wrongdoing in that incident, the memory was still fresh when Operation Sea Spirit placed her with a mixed nation battle group including the American destroyers Frank E Evans, Everett F Larson, and the James E Kyes, the New Zealand frigate Blackpool, and the English HMS Cleopatra. With four different navies and procedures, the commanding officer of the Melbourne, Captain John Stevenson held a dinner for the skippers of his five escorts at the start of the exercise. He had written instructions for procedures given to each ship and instructed that if an escort was to proceed to the plane guard position (starboard side aft of the carrier) that the destroyer would never turn into the direction of the carrier but away for safety. He also instructed that the minimum distance in this maneuver be 2,000 yards.

The Larson was the first to disregard these instructions. When proceeding to plane guard, she had turned in instead of out, but collision was avoided. Still, Stevenson reiterated his instructions to the five ships and increased minimum distance to 3,000 yards.

All of this was unknown to the aviation crews. What was known was that within a few days the exercise would be finished, and they would be sailing to Thailand. Prior to that happening, it was thought by the powers to be, to have cross training so the shipboard types would understand the aviators and the aviators would understand the obstacles faced by the black shoe navy. To that end, HS-6 pilot Rudy Cartwright, was high lined to the Evans from the Kearsarge on June 2nd. At first, he was scheduled to go into port with the Evans, but after a busy morning and afternoon of cross deck training, Cartwright wished to be back at the squadron to attack the mountains of paperwork produced by the modern militaries and asked for transit back to HS-6. Instead of facing the perils of the high line, HS-6 had sent a helo commanded by Doug Heggie and Rudy was back in the squadron ready room where he was promptly added to the flight schedule. To welcome him back, he had a flight at 0300 with Gordy Thomas. Indeed, the Navy has its own way of making you feel needed.

On the night of June 2, the Melbourne group was involved in ASW exercises and was preparing to launch her S-2 Tracker aircraft when she instructed the Evans to take up plane guard position. At the time, the Evans was forward of the Melbourne and to her port side. So, to take up plane guard position, the watch officers on the Evans ordered the helmsman to turn to starboard, a heading that would cross the path of the Melbourne, thereby going against the instructions of Captain Stevenson. The Melbourne sent a radio message to the Evans that she was on a collision course, which the Evans merely acknowledged. Seeing that the destroyer did not act, Captain Stevenson ordered his helm to hard over to port and sounded the collision alarm by the ship's siren and radio. However, that was not enough. At 03:15, the bow of the Melbourne knifed through the Evans, separating the bow section from the rest of the ship. The bow sank immediately.

Cartwright, aloft prior to the collision, was unaware of the happenings. Soon after he lifted off with Thomas, they were given a different heading to what they had been briefed on. Regardless, they flew along that heading for twenty minutes until they arrived at a spot that "was lit up like Times Square during New Year's Eve." Cartwright wondered what was going on. Though they were given search vectors to look for survivors, Cartwright, Thomas, and his crew were still in the dark of what had transpired. He reported later that he believed a plane had impacted with the Melbourne as he had seen debris in the water.

As the day ended, Cartwright noticed a small craft and a funnel in the water, and thought it was a fleet tug, but one of the crew informed him that it was part of a destroyer. The pilots flew closer, and the crew identified the stern as the Evans, the same ship Cartwright was aboard a few hours prior, and the same ship he would have been aboard now if it wasn't for the Navy and its love for producing paperwork.

Ken Burns had been on a submarine screening exercise when the collision occurred. He had launched prior to midnight and was ecstatic that a "good moon" allowed the pilots to find a horizon in the distance, which he called a LooCom moon, a reference to a flying condition God reserved for Lcdr's and above. Whereas a black moonless night was referenced as the junior officer "black hole".

Burns, with Tom Hutchinson as co-pilot, had experienced the normal challenges. The fire-warning T-handles on his aircraft, Indian Gal 59, had been going off. He had seen this before and was not alarmed as it usually occurred when the engine compartments did not contain airflow sufficient to cool the system due to maximum weight and a no-wind condition. When that happened, Burns would call for an up hoist to the sonar operators and would bore a few holes in the sky allowing the cooling winds of forward flight to cool the system, and then continue with the sonar mission after the T- handle lights dimmed and went back to normal. With time, they had burned enough fuel (1,000 pounds per hour) reducing the weight of the aircraft, which then allowed them to finish the dip cycles. Burns recalled that it was after that that they heard the call: "Wildcat, (Kearsarge call sign) to RTB (return to base) for a hot refuel and new assignment." Great," thought Burns, "we just get light enough to go through full cycles and we get pumped full to the max again."

Burns, like Cartwright, was not informed of his new mission. It was only when they reached the new coordinates and Melbourne had assigned him a search area that they knew they were in a SAR mission.

"We crisscrossed our area and saw a lot of debris, but never any survivors. There were several motor whale boats in the water, and more and more helos began to arrive on the scene," Burns recalled.

"We eventually saw an odd-looking craft; it looked like some yard craft or a cable layer sitting dead in the water. It was odd looking stack canted forward, hardly any ship aft of the stack, a 5-inch mount up front of the bridge, some sort of cable hanging over the bow. Eventually we had enough light that we air taxied over to the ship. We were absolutely stunned to finally recognize it as the aft section of the Evans. We continued to search for survivors (never finding any) and eventually returned to Kearsarge."

The duty officer in the squadron Ready Room at the time was Roger Wharton. He would later recall that the ready room was always a haze of smoke from pipes and cigarettes. The standby crew was asleep, as was most of the squadron, and he was making mundane log entries when the phone rang. "This is operations. There has been a collision at sea, prepare to launch all available helicopters."

Frank E Evans, stern section, the morning of June 3, HS-6 helos swarming above. USN photo

Meanwhile, it was a beehive of activity aboard the Melbourne. The Melbourne had stopped immediately after the collision, and lowered its boats and life rafts, while its members dove into the debris-covered waters to save American sailors. The Melbourne maneuvered itself abeam of the stern section and lashed the two ships together as the Aussies aided the Americans to safety. Then its band mustered to provide diversion for the shocked crew. All the survivors were located within the first twelve minutes, prior to any of the Indian Gal helos arriving on the scene. Unfortunately, not all the men survived.

Since the loss of the Sullivan brothers in WW2, brothers were prohibited from serving on the same ship. That policy was reversed to allow the three Sage brothers from Niobrara, Nebraska to serve on the Evans. Sadly, all three were among the 74 men lost, most of whom were in the bow section.

The Evans was towed to Naval Station Subic Bay and stripped of all valuable gear, prior to being decommissioned, and used for target practice.

HS-6 would be commended for her efforts by the Commander of Antisubmarine Warfare Group 1 thus:

1. *While participating in the joint SEATO exercise SEA SPIRIT in the South China Sea, the HMAS Melbourne (CVS- 21) and*

the USS Frank E Evans (DD-754) were involved in a disastrous collision at 0315 on June 3, 1969, some 40 miles from the USS Kearsarge. At approximately 0340 Helicopter Anti-Submarine Squadron Six personnel were alerted to the call from Flag Officer Commanding Her Majesties Australian Fleet, for assistance in the form of all available helicopter support. The response was accomplished in an astonishing short period of time.

2. *The ready alert aircraft was expeditiously manned and airborne in less than ten minutes. Quickly following four more aircraft were spotted and readied for launch. These aircraft were launched in approximately twenty minutes from initial notification, and then four more aircraft were placed in the ready alert status. The time required to complete the entire evolution was less than 45 minutes. Helicopter Squadron Six aircraft were rapidly on the scene contributing to the search for survivors and evacuation of the injured which continued until dark on the evening of June 3.*

3. *The leadership, devotion to duty, personal dedication and rapid response exhibited by Squadron officers and men enabled Helicopter Anti-Submarine Six to perform in a superb manner during this unforeseeable emergency. The innumerable tasks associated with search and rescue of survivors demanded outstanding professional performance and personal sacrifices by each member of the squadron. The untiring effort, sound judgement, and can-do spirit demonstrated by Helicopter Anti-Submarine Squadron Six produced timely and effective results and contributed greatly to the rescue effort.*
4. *Accordingly, I wish to personally commend your command and extend a hearty "well done."*

J.H. King Jr. (VADM)

For the younger enlisted that had been on the previous cruise, the loss of the Evans was particularly sour. The non-military would not understand the bond between the two groups of enlisted sailors, but they were fighting buddies. Somewhere in the past, no one knows how it started or why, but the junior enlisted men of the two commands would often brawl in liberty ports. The author witnessed this on several occasions. In HS-6, it usually occurred in the Line Division, those maintainers that wore the dirty colored, grease soaked, jet fuel smelling, brown flight deck shirts. The Evans involved were usually the white skinned, red seaman stripe wearing, denizens of the bowels of the ship, the snipes.

No one noticed why it started, or why it continued, except it was tradition. The only thing needed to keep it going was for one of the groups to see the shoulder patch that read Frank E Evans or Helantisubron 6 and the fight would be on. Usually, petty officers above the rank of third class avoided the tradition either out of fear of losing a stripe, or because the adage "with age comes wisdom" finally had a modicum of truth. Regardless, what the average reader will not understand is that there was a bond, and when the Evans was lost, it hurt.

Notes:
Rudy Cartwright notes about the Frank Evans incident. Raunchy Redskins site
Ken Burns notes on the Frank Evans Incident
Roger Wharton notes on the Frank Evans Incident
Admiral King ASW Group 1, Letter of Commendation

CHAPTER 20

TIDBITS OF A MEMORY BEGINNING TO FAIL

While I was writing this, I had trouble understanding what I wanted the reader to take with them. Now, after pecking away with both fingers, index on the right and the express yourself finger on the left, I think what I wish to convey is how much I respected the men I served with. That these guys were special. We grew up hearing about the greatest generation; well, these were the greatest guys in my generation.

Whether you were in on one of the many courageous rescues in the book or not largely fell to chance. When some poor attack or fighter pilot ate a SAM or ground fire while you were on duty, your crew would inevitably be tasked by Harbor Master to go get them. Some of our best guys were not tasked.

Many I have spoken to asked if I was going to include the space flights the squadron recovered. Initially, I wasn't going there, but here in "Tidbits", I'll dabble the toe to test the water.

Everyone on the Westpac cruises remembers a bronze plaque embedded in the flight deck where Faith-7, the last of the Mercury launches was hoisted aboard the Kearsarge, and astronaut Gordon Cooper emerged. The underwater demolition team that had trained tirelessly to secure the capsule had been delivered by Indian Gal Airlines.

After our 66 cruise, a few of our flight crews were again preparing to recover the first Apollo Mission. Terry Hall remembered the short flight from Ream Field to the strand at Coronado, where they would board "very fit, very tan" swimmers from the UDT/SEAL training site and remarked that they appeared as they had just come off the set on the latest Annette Funicello beach movie. "At the time, I was a tad upset at being assigned this, I was just getting ready to be discharged and head home, and here we had another short cruise prior to me leaving, but the fire changed that." The fire he was referring was the Apollo

1 fire that took the lives of Gus Grissom, Ed White, and Roger Chaffee.

If you look at the picture from the 1966 cruise commemorating the 21,000 landings on the Old Kearsarge, you will see a crew in a nutshell comprised of the veteran pilot, the junior officer, and two enlisted crewmen.

Grulkowski, Petrovich, Sanders, Grigsby 1966 after being the 21,000 landing on the USS Kearsarge. Photo courtesy HS-6 Raunchy Redskins

We'd often joke about Sanders, the tall good looking kid 3rd from left having Hollywood looks, and I having a face made for radio.

Nevertheless, Dan Sanders was not a career sailor. He had married his high school sweetheart, Annette, and after four years and two deployments away from his wife, it was time to be a full-time husband. Dan, however, did not leave his courage behind when he left the squadron. When he was home, he happened across an armed robbery, and not being a man to cower back and let some other man step up, stepped in to protect the store personnel, only to receive a shot in the head for his efforts.

He survived the blast but had memory loss. One day, he went to Annette and explained that he had no memories of what he did for fun before the shooting. Did he hunt, fish, play golf, what did he enjoy doing. Annette, not just beautiful but bright as well, explained that his hobby was to be her perfect husband, and he did so better than anyone could imagine.

She explained that she wouldn't change a thing about him, as he was the ideal husband. He would come home and do laundry and loved ironing his shirts with the two creases in the front just like when he was in the squadron. He even enjoyed doing the dishes, as it left him feeling clean. To work off stress, he would vacuum as the humming noise calmed him. And every so often he would cook a nice dinner for the two of them, complete with a single red rose on the table.

As time passed, Dan healed, and his memory began to return, but he had no memories of all the things Annette said he loved to do. More time passed, and he had visions of fishing creeping into his mind, but still no thoughts of doing dishes. He brought this to Annette, and she couldn't help but laugh. Then, he knew his beautiful wife had put one over. Indeed, her beauty was matched by her sense of humor, and they both laughed.

The two of them told Terry Hall and I this story at our squadron reunion in 2015 at a small Inn in Colonial Williamsburg. They were still laughing at the joke she had played so many years ago and were also celebrating being married for more than fifty years.

Our squadron was full of larger-than-life characters. One of my favorites was George Armstrong, who was a jet engine mechanic, and a good one. He was also fiercely brave, as a descendent of warriors would be.

He joined the Navy and left his home reservation in the American Northwest. Though he'd been a keen witness to the poverty of reservation life, he did not let that change him.

If George had a weakness, it was drink. Simply put, he enjoyed sloshing a few when he was off duty (Though at my last meeting with George, it was a habit he no longer had). During one of our liberty calls, George had thrown back a few and was becoming a tad unmanageable. Regardless, his fellow crewmen managed to get him back to the Kearsarge without damage to either his rank or the personnel around him. His flying partner, Jimmy Conrad, reminding him that George Armstrong was part of the name of a famous cavalry officer, George Armstrong Custer, bestowed the Indian sounding name of Crazy Pigeon, and it stuck.

Out of the squadrons' love and respect for this man, we would have a Crazy Pigeon delegation where one of us midline petty officers accompanied George at liberty to keep him out of trouble. It was a difficult task.

The night I drew Crazy Pigeon patrol in Japan, we walked into town, proceeded to a Marine Bar, (Crazy Pigeon idea), and proceeded to order a round. I ordered my Coke (dutiful to my task), and Crazy Pigeon ordered a Tory and Mizu, (Japanese whisky and water). Somehow, I don't know why, but the water part did not seem to function in the body as well as the Tory's.

We had been there perhaps half an hour when George stood on the table and announced to the Marines assembled that he and his buddy (me) could whip all in the bar. I quickly urged him down and made alternate grinning and pleading looks to the Marines in the smoke-filled joint. However, things resumed to normal, and we were discussing our homes, the squadron, flying, and helicopters in general. I thought my night of Crazy Pigeon Patrol was progressing fine until I needed to visit the benjo (Japanese toilet that consisted of a hole in the ground where you practice urine strafing attacks while attempting to keep ones shoes dry).

Upon returning from said ensuite conditions, Crazy Pigeon again stood, this time on his chair, and in a loud voice announced the lack of chastity among Marine wives, girlfriends, sisters, etc. My attempt to get to Pigeon was interrupted when I got blindsided by a haymaker from the direction of the juke box. What before had sounded like the best the Righteous Brothers could sing, now had a curious ringing noise from deep inside my head. I managed to get my head off the floor to see Crazy Pigeon heavily outnumbered but still swinging wildly with a laughter that must have come from whatever the Blackfeet call hell.

Thankfully, the owner of the bar called Shore Patrol as soon as Crazy Pigeon began his speech. Thankfully, again, they were close and arrived quickly. They were decent enough to drive us to the dispensary and allow the duty corpsman to shove cotton up our nose to staunch some of the bleeding.

After we left the medical facilities, we were taken straight to the Kearsarge. Walking up the gangway, we saluted the stern, in honor of Old Glory, saluted the Officer of the Deck, and asked in our best sailor voice for permission to come aboard. The junior officer manning the quarter deck took a long look at our appearance. Our whites were no longer white and still had shoe polish in places where the Marines threw the leather into us. Pigeon's jumper had one arm dangling as the thread connecting it to the torso had been pulled apart. He stared for a long moment, shook his head, and answered, "Permission granted to come aboard, leaving this ship may be more difficult." He then assigned a master-at-arms, the ships policeman, to us and we were escorted to the squadron ready room.

The junior officer who was the squadron duty officer was less than thrilled at being called. As we waited, I remember looking at my sleeve where I had sewn on the rank of petty officer second class not many months prior. I stared at the spread eagle of the rank badge, wondering if it would survive, or if I would be busted down to airman status.

I looked at George, and shook my head while asking, "Why did we just do this, why?"

The big guy just thumped me on the back and with a hearty laugh said, "Now you know just how helpless Custer felt." He was still laughing when the junior officer arrived.

Being the sober one, I tried my best to explain truthfully what had happened. I had a glimmer of hope when I saw him try to stifle a grin. Then we were confined to our berthing section until the skipper made a final determination. We sailed from port soon after and the incident was forgotten.

At our reunion in 2017, George and I tried to recall the junior officer that had duty that night. The night was hazy to George, and he didn't remember everything but had brief memories of individual instances and grinned when those memories flowed over him, and I was thankful I endured the incident with my rank intact, and the passage of time softened my memory. Ron Clarke, one of George's pilots was also at the reunion and after fifty years, the bond was just as strong. I flew hundreds of hours with our squadron, but one of my most intense experiences was my night with the Crazy Pigeon patrol.

Two other memorable characters were Bernie Riley and Ski with an N. We English descendants had trouble with the various Polish names, therefore we had a Ski with a K, Kozawkowski and Ski with an N, Niederoski. Bernie and Ski with an N were best buddies but would fight every time we arrived at a liberty port. Bernie would always claim to be the next winner of the bout and like death and taxes was always promptly pummeled. Later in the evening, we would find the two, sharing brews, uniforms disheveled, Bernie's eyes nearly shut, welts on his cheeks, and dried blood on his upper lip. We would inquire out of courtesy how the battle went, and Bernie would always tell us, next time boys, I'll get him. Next time was like the movie Ground Hog Day: same ending, different setting.

I was berthed with the line crew, the division of the squadron that was responsible for the daily maintenance, cleaning, positioning, and securing the aircraft. Flying was also part of my duties.

The line crews were the baseline for the squadron, which consisted mostly of junior petty officers and airmen. The corporate world would call it an entry level position, but the rest of the squadron just called us, line pukes.

We wore brown long-sleeved pullover shirts, usually adorned with grease stains, oil spills, salty sweat rings from the arm pits—just your average dress for dinner wear. We, like the rest of the squadron, worked twelve-hour shifts, seven days a week. The dayshift was normally tasked with launching recovering, aiding in fueling, and being the brakeman when a helo was being moved.

Night was usually the shift for cleaning. Fresh water was always in short supply on the old Essex-classed carriers, so cleaning was done with cans of waterless cleaner, and mountains of rags. The salt air was highly corrosive to the skin of the aircraft making corrosion control a high priority.

Off duty, there was a table in each berthing compartment meant for paperwork, letters home, etc. but normally fielding a pinochle game. Besides that, most of us found fun wherever we could find or make it.

A ship rolling in light or moderate seas could be trouble for a 20,000-pound helo. To secure it, the plane captains would use heavy tie down chains on each main gear and the tail. When one was particularly bored, he would spread the tie down chains in the widest possible pattern, going a pad eye farther than needed. Then they were secured and tightened. All that remained was to crawl into the darkened helo, maintain silence, and wait for the inevitable thump that would come when an unsuspecting passerby hit his shins on the thick chains. This tactic was usually used when in the hanger deck immediately over the Marine berthing compartment. The language some of those Marines used when their shins would strike the chains would make a chief blush.

One other favorite diversion came when the ship would take on stores from a supply vessel. To do this, working parties were formed to help store the goods. Obviously, when food stuffs for officers came aboard a tax was taken. A box of canned fruit, fruit juices, or nuts hidden away or tossed down a storage hole was always welcome. Flights into Danang were opportunities to add to our ration fare by bringing beer back to the Kearsarge. Our M-60 ammo was linked together into 2,000 round links and placed in a 20mm ammo can. By chance, two cases of beer could also fit in said 20mm can. Therefore, all one had to do was dump the ammo onto the flight line and load up four cases of beer. This fun ended when the squadron had a SAR scramble held up for a few minutes trying to locate the cans with ammo. If one could find an Aussie digger hat while in Danang, that was excellent barter material.

Chiefs…that rank that invokes immediate respect. The navy is the only US service where the top three enlisted ranks wear a different uniform from the bottom six ranks. While we were dressed in blue dungarees, chambray shirt, or flight line shirt, the chiefs wore khaki, same as the commissioned officers. Dress uniforms were officer type except for the chiefs' rating badge being on the upper arm and not stripes at the wrist. The chiefs had their own mess, and quarters—one that was off limits without permission to enter. Great histories record wonderful heroic stories of naval heroes, Farragut, John Paul Jones, Dewey, Nimitz, Spruance, Lawrence, etc. But be assured when these giants issued orders, it was chief petty officers that got it done.

We lived and worked in a Navy more in tune with WW2 then the present. No cell phones, no computers, and navigation was by TACAN and vectors. Our spaces were not for the PC generation. They were cigarette smoke filled, non airconditioned in the equatorial heat, and so close-quartered that when you woke up you had the person's feet next to your face. It was head to toe sleeping or as we would say today social distancing. We were a different group, that had been raised in the shadow of WW2 and lived on those expectations. In the mess deck, we talked to each other and didn't stare at our phones. Ashore a fight might brew up in an instance, and the combatants would be sharing a cool one an hour later.

Money was plentiful for most, as we usually had no place to spend it, except for the occasional poker or tonk game. For those that run short of money, there was always a loan shark available with the standard rate of five for seven (If you borrowed five dollars you would pay back seven dollars the following payday). Of course, gambling and loan sharking were strictly against policy, but *c'est la vie, c'est la guerre.*

In 2017, we were able to meet the squadron that was once ours, Helicopter Sea Combat Six, and I think we were all impressed by the new breed of sailors, both men and women. We loved the new birds and their expanded capabilities. (They had real chaff dispensers vice, a cardboard tube that the crewmen would open at one end to shake aluminum "gum wrappers" at the enemy. The enlisted men I spoke to were better educated (no high school dropouts), motivated professionals. The language was cleaner, the uniforms sharper, and computers certainly have changed maintenance. The new insignia was the same as the old except the submarine trapped in the 6 figure was now gone.

Another item that was gone was cigarette smoke. In the squadron on the Kearsarge, our ready room was so filled with smoke the London fog might have been envious. Cigarettes were merely $1.10 per carton unless you bought Chesterfields on sale for $.50 a carton. At those prices, damaging your health was affordable and everyone smoked. John Wayne and doctors advertised cigarettes in print and television ads. No, the new navy although much slimmer than the one thousand ships in our navy including twenty carriers, is much more capable with all the new technology.

After I left the service, I was in contact with veterans of other branches of the service. I realized how special our officers were. They, for the most part, led because we willingly followed them and not because they had rank.

In the Navy, there was a legend of a mythical bird, a bird so special that he could fly at an ever-increasing speed and an ever-decreasing circle, until he flew so fast and in such a sharp turn that he flew up his own rear and disappeared from the face of the earth. This special creature was the Geezelbird, and yes, we had one officer we named the Geezelbird. However, he was the exception.

We also had Al Fox, our skipper in the 67–68 deployment. For us that berthed in the lower decks, that could read daily of the college kids constantly voiceful against the war and those in uniform that served in the war, for us that saw newsreels of Jane Fonda sitting on a NVA anti-aircraft mount grinning and joking while she pretended to shoot down our fellow Americans, our morale needed uplifting. Cdr Fox gave us that lift. He was quite a guy and took command at a critical time. He last led us in a Veterans Day Parade at Colonial Williamsburg in 2015, he passed not long after in San Angelo, Texas.

While we were gone on those two Westpac cruises, America and its attitudes towards the war began to change and with that its attitude towards the warrior was also changing. The new President, Richard Nixon called our supporters the silent majority. The loud minority impacted how we were viewed.

However, I wouldn't have missed my time with the "old six" for anything. They were the best squadron mates a man could have and the best men I have ever known.

I was angered when young men left for Canada to avoid service and was angrier still when President Carter gave them amnesty. Today, I feel sorry for them, because they never had the opportunity to bond with their fellow countrymen in a way that only warriors know. To paraphrase an old Texas playwright, Billy Bob Shakespeare:

We few, We happy few, We Band of Brothers
For whom so ever will shed his blood with me
Is my brother, now and until the end of time.

Notes:

Conversations with Dan and Annette Sanders in 2015 in Colonial Williamsport
Conversations with Terry Hall ongoing
Conversations with George Armstrong, San Diego 2017
King Henry V, William Shakespeare
Special thanks to Ken Burns and Ron Milam for keeping history alive.

Ingram Content Group UK Ltd.
Milton Keynes UK
UKHW020644220523
422140UK00015B/547